TALES FROM THE
TITANS
SIDELINE

JIM WYATT

www.SportsPublishingLLC.com

Director of production: Susan M. Moyer
Acquisitions editor: Dean Reinke
Developmental editor: Elisa Bock Laird
Photo editor: Erin Linden-Levy
Project manager: Greg Hickman
Copy editor: Cynthia L. McNew
Imaging and dust jacket design: Dustin Hubbart
Marketing manager: Monica Heckman

ISBN: 1-58261-618-3

Printed in the United States.

CONTENTS

PREFACE

At first, it all seemed like a dream. For an NFL fan in Nashville, it was simply too good to be true.

Yet here they were—Nashville mayor Phil Bredesen and Houston Oilers owner Bud Adams—standing side by side at a reception at the Wildhorse Saloon in downtown Nashville, talking about the exclusive negotiating agreement they had just signed.

It was August 11, 1995.

"There are absolutely no deal-killers on either side so far," Bredesen said as he introduced Adams to about 250 political and business leaders from across the state. "It will be Tennessee's team, not just Nashville's team."

Then Adams spoke up.

"We're ready to come here and get it done," Adams said. "Nashville and the State of Tennessee, including Memphis and Chattanooga and your other great cities in the state, are a damn good football state and cities. I don't have to tell you how good of fans you are. You know how good of fans you are. We want to kind of join with you over here if we can."

☆☆☆☆☆☆

After all the discussions, after the stadium site had been picked, after the personal seat licenses had gone on sale, and after the NFL owners had approved the Oilers' move to Nashville, there was still something holding the move back: the public's vote.

It came on May 7, 1996, after weeks of arguing back and forth between the two sides.

Opponents of the move, after first gathering enough signatures to call for the special referendum, picketed against it. They wore T-shirts and passed out "Vote No" signs. They tried their best to kill the deal.

After five years of sellouts, one has to wonder how many of those same folks go to the Coliseum on Sundays now. They'll never tell.

Yes, what started as a pipe dream less than a year earlier became a reality that day when voters in Davidson County helped make the move possible. The uncertified results that night: 59 percent for the Oilers' deal, 41 percent against.

Organizers of a "Vote Yes" campaign before the election passed out 500,000 bumper and lapel stickers, 30,000 yard signs, 4,000 T-shirts, 2,000 caps, and 600 mugs.

The night of May 7 they all celebrated together in Nashville. Mike McClure, the Oilers' executive vice president, was presented with a coach's whistle to thank him for his efforts. Bredesen got an MVP "game ball."

"Wow!" said Bredesen, standing before a huge crowd of supporters. "You did it! You did it! You really did it! Thank you!"

☆☆☆☆☆☆

Before long, the NFL kicked off in Tennessee, but in time more hurdles would need to be cleared.

Although Adams was willing to move the Oilers out of Houston, for the longest time he was reluctant to change the team's name.

While crowds were embarrassingly low at the Liberty Bowl in Memphis during the 1997 season and interest in Nashville was luke-warm at best, the name debate remained a hot-button issue in the state and in the NFL.

From the very beginning, fans began pressing Adams for a change. He made it clear, however, any change in identity or appearance wouldn't occur until the team moved into a new stadium in downtown Nashville in 1999, if then. NFL commissioner Paul Tagliabue didn't disagree with the owner's logic.

Few in Nashville, however, agreed with that line of thinking.

For at least a while, Adams kept playing up to the folks in Memphis, even though they weren't going to watch his team play.

The Oilers averaged just 28,028 fans in eight games played at the Liberty Bowl in 1997, and a good deal of those fans made the three-hour drive from Nashville each week.

"Down here in Memphis they don't mind," Adams said at the time. "They think the 'Oilers' is a pretty good name. I haven't heard anything against it."

Again, it was a different story in Nashville, even though Adams seemed almost oblivious to the desires of the fans. In a September 1997 poll conducted by *The Tennessean* in Nashville, 83 percent of voters said the Oilers should change their nickname. Folks were getting more outspoken by the day.

Finally, in July 1998, Adams buckled. The clincher was when Tagliabue agreed to retire the name Oilers and allow the franchise to retain and protect its 39-year history. No team in Houston—now home to the NFL's Texans—will ever have the option of resurrecting the name Oilers.

The search for a new name for Tennessee's team began.

Since then the team has been a "Titanic" success, and today the Titans are the hottest thing going in Nashville.

The games are sold out, they have marquee players, and they've been successful, with playoff appearances in four of the first five years since moving into the Coliseum.

Indeed, the move has been a success, just like Adams envisioned it would when he was first introduced to the city that summer night in 1995.

ACKNOWLEDGMENTS

I would like to thank my wonderful wife, Stephanie, and my two children—Rhett and Sydney—for their help and patience with this project, but also for bringing so much happiness into my life. No words can describe what the three of you mean to me.

I'd also like to thank my parents, Randall and Kay Wyatt, for your love and support over the years. I hope my children will always be as proud of me as I am of the two of you.

Thanks to my brother, Vince, for being such a good friend.

Also, thanks to my colleagues at *The Tennessean*, especially Paul Kuharsky and Jeff Legwold, who bent over backward to show a rookie NFL reporter the ropes back in 1999 and also for their continued support, knowledge, and encouragement.

And thanks to the former and current Tennessee Titans players, coaches, and support staff who took the time to share their memories and thoughts. I've truly enjoyed being around to experience the ups and downs of the past five years.

CHAPTER ONE

BECOMING THE TITANS

TITANS IT IS

In November 1998, it was announced that the Oilers would officially become the Titans in 1999.

Owner Bud Adams and the group of business leaders from around Tennessee he put together as an advisory council chose the name Titans over Pioneers and Tornadoes. Other names that were considered by the 13-member council: Ambush; Bandits; Blitz; Bobcats; Commanders; Conquerors; Copperheads; Cougars; Cruisers; Daredevils; Dynamos; Firestorm; Fury; Generals; Legends; Marauders; Nighthawks; Pioneers; Power; Presidents; Rampage; Rapids; Rattlers; Renegades; River Bandits; Siege; Smokies; Sound; Stallions; Stampede; Stingers; Talons; Tempest; Thunder; Tornadoes; Tradition; Troopers; Vipers.

The news disappointed Bill Bledsoe, who with friends and family invested about $30,000 in a campaign to see the Oilers become the Tennessee Copperheads. The campaign picked up some steam but was nipped by Bud.

"One of the strong recommendations the advisory council made was no snakes or reptiles," Adams explained. "That eliminated Copperheads and Vipers. My apologies to the herpetologists."

AN EARLY CHRISTMAS PRESENT

Fans already knew their team would be the Titans. But now they wanted to see the logo.

Three days before Christmas in 1998, on a cold day in Nashville, the Titans unveiled their new logo at a press conference at the Parthenon in Centennial Park.

Inside a white tent, it was unveiled—a white circle with a tail of blue and red fire. Inside the circle—the three stars of Tennessee and a metallic T with sharp points.

"It will be a winner with the fans and a proud association for our state," governor Don Sundquist said at the ceremony.

The Oilers said the flames represented the fire of the Titans and the stars the state's three distinct regions.

Initially, fans looked at the logo and wondered. But it didn't take long for it to be a big hit. Merchandise started flying off the shelves at area stores, and fans at the upcoming game against the Vikings received a Titan towel bearing the logo.

More than 100 logos were created for owner Bud Adams to examine before he selected the one that still remains in the side of the team's white helmets.

"I like [the logo] a lot," tackle Brad Hopkins said. "The colors were a surprise for me. They kept that sky blue in there, we can't get away from that."

CAN I HAVE A DO-OVER?

Nothing about the Oilers' move from Houston to Tennessee was flawless, so coach Jeff Fisher's faux pas at his postgame press conference after the team's first win in Memphis didn't come as a complete surprise.

The Tennessee Oilers' 24-21 overtime win over the Raiders at the Liberty Bowl in Memphis was something worth celebrating. Running back Eddie George had 216 yards rushing in the game, and the Oilers won it on a 33-yard kick by Al Del Greco.

After the game, the players ran back on the field and thanked the fans.

Fisher, like everyone else, was excited. Before long, he was a bit embarrassed.

With television cameras and reporters waiting for him, Fisher entered the tiny interview room with a sweat-soaked shirt and a smile on his face.

"On behalf of the entire Oilers organization, I would like to take this opportunity to award our first game ball to governor Don Sundquist from the Houston Oilers, uhh, the Tennessee Oilers organization," Fisher said before stopping himself for a moment.

The smile stayed, but his face turned to a shade of red.

"... I was hoping this was going to go better than that."

THE LAST STRAW

It took the biggest home crowd of the 1997 season to make the Oilers realize Memphis wasn't for them—in more ways that one. To have only 17,737 fans turn out for a September contest against the Ravens was embarrassing.

Things were even worse when the Oilers played at home next—just 17,071 showed up at the Liberty Bowl to watch the Oilers beat the Bengals.

But what happened at the final game of the season against the Pittsburgh Steelers took the cake. It was enough to finally convince owner Bud Adams it was time to leave Memphis once and for all. It came not too long after he uttered these words: "I said I was going to be here for two years and I plan to be here unless the bottom falls out. And I don't see that happening."

On December 21, 1997, the bottom officially dropped out.

True, 50,677 fans turned out to watch the Oilers beat the Steelers. But the majority of the crowd was decked out in black and gold, something that left the players shaking their heads.

"We got more boos in the Liberty Bowl here than we had probably up in Pittsburgh," tackle Brad Hopkins said. "That to me is incredible."

Even though part of the separation process would have to involve dealing with the headaches of working through a two-year lease with the Liberty Bowl, after the game Adams for the first time indicated it would probably be worth it.

The Oilers' new stadium in Nashville wasn't scheduled to be ready until the 1999 season, but Vanderbilt Stadium in Nashville sure seemed like a good option all of a sudden.

"We don't want to offend Memphis," Oilers

— **TITAN TALK** —

"We didn't know we were going to play Pittsburgh on the road twice this year."

—Eddie George,
running back

Fans watch the Tennessee Oilers beat the Oakland Raiders in overtime.
The Liberty Bowl turned out to be a less than welcoming venue
as the Oilers waited for their stadium in Nashville to be completed.
Vincent Laforet/Getty Images

guard Kevin Donnalley said. "It's not their fault, but if we can do it, let's go."

Two months later, the Oilers reached an agreement with the Shelby County Sports Authority and Memphis Park Commission to be released from the final year of their lease with the Liberty Bowl. Less than two weeks later, the team reached an agreement to play at Vanderbilt Stadium for the 1998 season.

While the crowds at Vanderbilt were nothing to brag about, the memories of Memphis and the black-and-gold sea of Pittsburgh fans were a thing of the past.

"How would you feel if most of the people are yelling for the Steelers?" Adams said. "I don't think it feels good to have 60 percent of the people for the Steelers, 70 percent. We're supposed to be the home team. They don't seem to care for the Oilers."

Truth be told, they never did.

LESS THAN IDEAL SETUP

The Titans moved into their state-of-the-art training facility near downtown Nashville prior to the 1999 season, but before that their working conditions were far from ideal.

During their first two seasons in Nashville, the Oilers' practice facility was composed of the back half of a pediatrician's complex with portable trailers behind it.

They waited several months into their first season until a divider was put in that allowed the offense and defense to hold simultaneous meetings in the main trailer. Before that, the offense would kick reporters out of the media trailer for meetings. Players occasionally left playbooks and game plans behind.

Needless to say, it wasn't a great situation for anyone.

The practice setup was just as bad. Kicker Al Del Greco and the special teams were oftentimes responsible for dragging portable goalposts to the spot where they wanted them. A practice field with no drainage system would sometimes get so waterlogged that the Oilers were forced to run sideline to sideline instead of end zone to end zone.

When NFL Players Association head Gene Upshaw got news of it all, he sent a strongly worded letter to NFL commissioner Paul Tagliabue complaining about the facility, among other things.

Upshaw was also upset about the team's travel plans for home games that were being played in Memphis that year. And so were many of the players and their wives.

The plan that year did not allow members of the team to travel home to Nashville with their families from games. While the team flew to and from Memphis, players' families rode buses that left Sunday mornings and returned Sunday night, oftentimes a few hours after the team's plane landed. Players were obligated to ride the team plane home. The players weren't happy.

"I don't expect [the players] to speak up, that's what I'm supposed to do," Upshaw said. "I don't want them to get in front of the train. They raised the issue with me, and I'll take it to the appropriate sources. I know all these things affect the way a player prepares himself to play. [Oilers coach Jeff] Fisher's lucky to win a game under these conditions ..."

In response to Upshaw's letter of complaint, owner Bud Adams promised things would get better. Adams said he actually felt the interim facility in Nashville was better than the one left behind in Houston.

Along the way, improvements were made, some bigger than others. For some players, even the tiniest steps seemed monumental.

A few weeks after Upshaw's letter to Tagliabue, for instance, at least a few players were overjoyed when a cappuccino/hot chocolate machine was added to the locker room. It was a sign that things were moving in the right direction.

"Once you get a cappuccino machine you know you've made the big time," Oilers punter Reggie Roby said.

THIS IS THE NFL?

It wasn't too long ago, however, when coach Jeff Fisher had to scramble just to get tape of an upcoming opponent. When his team first moved to Nashville, high school coaches had an easier time than the Oilers, who were competing with teams equipped with the latest technology.

Take this story, for example: It was the 1997 season, and the Oilers were four days away from a Thursday game at Cincinnati. It was a rare Sunday off since the team had just played the previous Thursday in Dallas.

But the Oilers had some unanswered questions about the Bengals. Cincinnati was suddenly beginning to score a lot of points under the direction of backup quarterback Boomer Esiason, a late-season fill-in for starter Jeff Blake.

Were the Bengals doing something different, perhaps using a no-huddle? Fisher needed answers, but with no satellite dish at their temporary facility, he couldn't even pick up the game to watch it.

What happened next is comical, but it shows the type of things the team had to go through during the transition.

Fisher called a sports bar just around the corner and asked the manager if he'd tape the Bengals-Eagles game for him. The manager agreed. Fisher went back to his office, went for a quick jog, and on the way back to the facility went by the sports bar to pick up the tape.

The crash course on the Cincinnati offense, which had scored 42 points that afternoon against the Eagles, was about to begin.

Or so Fisher thought.

On Fisher's way back to the facility, the weather began to change. Tornado warnings were in the area. Fisher decided to take a short cut. With the tape in hand, the head coach climbed a fence and rushed back to the trailers that were used for meetings rooms, only to find they had been evacuated.

After some searching, Fisher finally located his staff. The coaches were huddled in a nearby brick building that also housed some of the team officials.

"I walked in the brick building and was like, 'Well, I've got the tape!'" Fisher said. "I realized the things that we were doing at that point were different from what other teams were doing. I thought, 'Man, this is the NFL.'"

The Oilers ended up doing a decent job stopping Esiason that week. They didn't do so well stopping Bengals running back Corey Dillon, however. Dillon set the NFL's rookie rushing record with 246 yards in a 41-14 blowout win.

WHITE OUT

The Tennessee Oilers were set to play a nationally televised game in 1997 on Thanksgiving Day. The opponent: the Dallas Cowboys, in Texas Stadium, no less.

It was enough to make any youngster get sweaty palms, even some of the veterans. Oilers offensive lineman Kevin Donnalley could feel the tension leading up to the game. So after a flight from Nashville to Dallas, he thought it would be a good time to lighten the mood. It was the night before the game.

"There wasn't a looseness about us. You don't want to go care-free in to a game, but you need to not worry about things too much, TV and playing the Cowboys at home with the crowd," Donnalley said. "So I just took it as a challenge. I needed to step up and create a bit of an atmosphere where everybody could get a little laugh."

For $100, which he collected from some of his teammates, Donnalley mooned special teams coach Russ Purnell and several other Oilers in the team bus traveling alongside his at the Dallas-Fort Worth Airport.

Donnalley said he didn't need the money but took it just in case.

"Something like that you're not going to do for free, because if some certain guys see it, there could be a fine sitting in your locker the next day," he said.

The "bottom" line: Donnelley's plan might have worked. The Oilers beat the Cowboys 27-14 the next day. At the least, he deserved an assist.

START OF SOMETHING

Even before they were Titans, Tennessee's rivalry with the Jaguars was simmering.

The 1998 season perhaps offered a sign of things to come—and bad blood—for the two franchises.

In Jacksonville, T-shirts were ready and hats were printed in anticipation of the Jaguars clinching the AFC Central title during Week 14 of the 1998 season. But the Tennessee Oilers topped the Jaguars 16-13 on Al Del Greco's 41-yard field goal with four seconds left in the game.

"We heard they had their hats and T-shirts made up and ready to hand out," defensive back Steve Jackson said. "We told them to take their hats and shirts and put them back in the box."

The Jaguars ended up winning the AFC Central title, and the Oilers missed the playoffs after losing their final two games of the year. But the stage was set for 1999 and beyond in what has become one of Tennessee's biggest rivalries.

LAYING AN EGG

Things weren't great, but they were a whole lot better than they'd been.

The Memphis days were behind them, and the Oilers were ready for at least a fresher start in yet another home venue, this time at Vanderbilt Stadium.

After a victory in the season opener at Cincinnati in 1998, momentum was starting to pick up as the team returned for the home opener against the San Diego Chargers. The first regular-season game in Nashville was a sellout.

"It's the first time in a long time I've seen players walking around asking each other if they have extra tickets. Obviously from an organization standpoint, we're very thankful," coach Jeff Fisher said. "It's going to be a great ballgame, and it's been a long time, a real long time."

Then the Oilers went out and stunk up the joint.

Their 13-7 loss to the Chargers was a huge step back for a team begging for support at the time. And it came against a mediocre San Diego team with a rookie quarterback, Ryan Leaf.

Fans booed the Oilers during the game, and some quickly abandoned ship. It was an ominous start to say the least.

A PLACE TO START

It was hardly a blip on the NFL's radar.

But for the Tennessee Oilers and the city of Nashville, it was at least a start.

Tennessee's 44-14 thrashing of the Cincinnati Bengals on October 18, 1998, at Vanderbilt Stadium was the first victory for the team in Nashville since leaving Houston after the 1996 season and spending the 1997 season in Memphis at the Liberty Bowl.

In the win, the Oilers rolled up 515 yards and scored the most points in seven years. Quarterback Steve McNair threw for 277 yards and a touchdown and ran for another. The Oilers had lost their first two home games in Nashville.

"We talked about this before the game, that we had to establish a home field," safety Blaine Bishop said.

The Oilers ended up going 3-5 at Vanderbilt Stadium and 8-8 overall in 1998.

CHAPTER TWO

THE SUPER SEASON

A Sneak Preview

Many of them once called a deteriorating Astrodome home. They did the same for the aging Liberty Bowl in Memphis, as well as Vanderbilt Stadium.

So when the Titans toured their new stadium on the Cumberland River just a few months before its scheduled completion, they could hardly contain themselves.

"This definitely gives inspiration to everybody who's been around the organization the past three, four years," running back Eddie George said.

"We didn't have an identity. Now we have a stamp—who we are, what we are, where we are."

Coach Jeff Fisher and the entire team traveled in two buses to the downtown stadium for a sneak preview during a May minicamp prior to the 1999 season.

The players walked around like kids in a candy store. Some scooped up dirt, others pretended it was already Sunday in the fall as they imagined the turf.

In three months, they'd return in pads.

"You get a sense that there will be something different about this whole thing," offensive lineman Bruce Matthews said.

He was right.

> — **TITAN TALK** —
>
> "I'm dancing in the end zone already."
>
> —Yancey Thigpen, receiver

A GRAND OPENING

It was a preseason game, yes.

But to the Titans and the fans of Nashville, the team's August 27, 1999, contest against the Atlanta Falcons meant so much more.

Anyone who didn't believe that only had to look around the Coliseum to be convinced—country music artist Faith Hill was there to sing the national anthem. NFL commissioner Paul Tagliabue was in the building, and boxing announcer Michael Buffer announced the lineups. ESPN was there, and a raccoon named T-Rac made his official debut as the team's mascot.

But most importantly, the Titans were finally there, too. The playing days at the Astrodome in Houston, the Liberty Bowl in Memphis, and Vanderbilt Stadium were finally a thing of the past.

"We're at home now, finally after four years," owner Bud Adams said. "What else could you ask for? It's exhilarating, just exhilarating. ... It's everything I imagined it would be."

The Titans won their first ever game at the Coliseum by a 17-3 score. They started off with a bang. On their first play from scrimmage, quarterback Neil O'Donnell, playing for the injured

The Titans began building a home fan
base at the beginning of the 1999 season.
Andy Lyons/Getty Images

Steve McNair, connected with receiver Yancey Thigpen for a 48-yard completion.

It was the start of something special: The Titans won all eight regular-season home games in 1999. The preseason crowd of 65,729 qualified as the largest home crowd in the history of the franchise.

"I feel like we were playing in the Super Bowl," safety Blaine Bishop said. "The fan support is unbelievable. The place is rowdy. ..."

MAKING THE MOST
OF A SECOND OPPORTUNITY

It was just a preseason game, but Titans defensive line coach Jim Washburn nearly broke out in tears when he stood on the field in Kansas City in August 1999.

Washburn, regularly the most vocal coach on the practice field each day, takes no day for granted. His players often joke that he's always talking about how he's on the verge of getting fired. Even during a record-setting sack season for the Titans in 1999, he was on edge.

But it's only because of what Washburn went through to make it to the NFL.

Fifteen years ago, Washburn thought his coaching career was wrecked because of his role in a steroids scandal at the University of South Carolina in the 1980s. At one point he was financially broke, and he mowed grass at a golf course and drove a truck, hauling hog feed.

He reached the low point in 1989, when he was forced to resign from a job at Purdue after he was indicted in the South Carolina steroids scandal for helping players obtain steroids. He still remembers what he did at the Indianapolis airport that year, the day he left Purdue.

"I took all my football films, tapes, and cutups and threw them in a dumpster," he said. "I figured I'd never coach again."

Washburn served three years probation through a plea bargain, and he eventually got back into football with the minor-league Charlotte Barons. In 1999, the Titans ended up hiring Washburn, who they hoped would jump-start their defensive line.

With the help of rookie defensive end Jevon Kearse, Washburn delivered. The Titans improved from 30 sacks to a team-record 54 in his first season, and the next year broke that record with 55 sacks. The play of the defensive line has been one of the team's strengths over the past five years, although it took a big hit after the 2003 season when Kearse and defensive tackle Robaire Smith departed in free agency.

Titans defensive tackle Josh Evans once called Washburn "the spice in the gumbo, the ingredient we needed."

When the Titans traveled to Indianapolis to take on the Colts in the AFC playoffs during the 1999 season, Washburn saw the same dumpster he'd thrown his Purdue films into 10 years earlier.

"It brought tears to my eyes," Washburn said.

Just like spicy gumbo.

BETTER BRING THE COTTON BALLS INSTEAD

It took just three games for the Coliseum to get a reputation—for being loud.

And because of that, Rams coach Dick Vermeil also learned the rules.

Prior to the Titans-Rams regular-season game in 1999, the Rams planned for their offensive linemen to wear electronic earplugs that would muffle sounds other than the voice of their quarterback.

— TITAN TALK —

"Word's getting out that [the] Coliseum is a tough place to play, and we have to continue to build that home-field advantage, make it the toughest place to play in the NFL. This is the case where the 12th man altered the preparation for a game, which is a good sign, a compliment to our fans."

—Jeff Fisher, head coach

The only problem: it was illegal. So when the Titans found out about it via a news note on the Internet, they notified the league. The NFL then called the Rams to tell them to leave the electronic devices at home.

"I just didn't know there was a rule against it," an irritated Vermeil told reporters after learning the news. "I thought innovation was a part of the game. Tell Bud Adams to spring for something."

The Titans, of course, got a kick out of the whole thing. Then they encouraged the fans to get even louder for the game.

ON THE MAP

Before Super Bowl XXXIV, the Titans and Rams first squared off in the regular season.

It's arguably the day the Titans first caught the nation's attention. The Rams entered the Halloween contest in 1999 unbeaten and a team many thought untouchable. Quarterback Kurt Warner had already thrown 18 touchdown passes in six games, and the Rams had outscored their opponents by just under 26 points per game.

The Titans, meanwhile, were 5-1 and energized by the return of quarterback Steve McNair, who missed the previous five games after back surgery.

Before the biggest and most boisterous crowd to date at the Coliseum, the Titans jumped out to a 21-0 lead in the first quarter as McNair threw two touchdown passes and ran for another. The Rams outscored the Titans 21-3 in the second half, but the Titans held on for a 24-21 win and improved to 6-1.

"This was a statement game sent around the country," Titans fullback Lorenzo Neal said. "Everybody was talking about the Rams. Hey, the Titans are for real."

In time, they'd prove it again and again until the two teams met again in Atlanta.

Steve McNair led the Titans to a season to remember.
Donn Jones

SPOOKY DAY

It was Halloween at the Coliseum, and Fred Miller was spooked.

The offensive tackle was wearing a different costume then—a St. Louis Rams uniform. And the player freaking him out was none other than Titans defensive end Jevon Kearse.

The two players laugh about the events of the 1999 season now, Kearse more than Miller, of course. (After Miller signed with the Titans as an unrestricted free agent prior to the 2000 season, the two got to know each other a lot better.)

But what happened that Sunday afternoon in October was certainly no laughing matter for Miller.

In Kearse's rookie season, Miller lost his composure and got the worst end of his head-to-head matchup with Kearse, along with an earful from the crowd.

Miller committed six false starts and a holding penalty and watched Kearse record five tackles, a sack, two quarterback pressures, and a forced fumble in Tennessee's 24-21 win over the Rams.

"He might be jumping in his sleep," Kearse joked after the game. "His eyes were so big, just watching me. ... After a while, I just started looking at him and laughing at him, trying to get in his head."

It worked. To his credit, an embarrassed Miller stood at his locker and answered every question from reporters that afternoon. Looking back, he admitted that experience took a while to get over.

"I needed a couple of days to get through it," Miller said. "I went home and really just sat down with my family, looked at my son, and saw how he loved me and my wife. My dogs treated me great."

"Lucky to Be Alive"

Titans safety Marcus Robertson gave 10 years of his life to the Oilers/Titans organization.

On December 27, 1999, he felt lucky he didn't lose his life off the field.

Robertson was taking his motorcycle for a spin, something he regularly did each week to make sure the battery stayed charged during the winter months, when he lost control roughly 400 yards from his home.

He initially tried to lift the bike up and get it home. But with blood running down his face, he decided just to jog home so he could get to the hospital as soon as possible.

Robertson needed 150 stitches and had extensive plastic surgery. Initially, he was reluctant to return to Baptist Sports Park because of his appearance, but Titans coach Jeff Fisher talked him into it. Robertson said it helped his healing process.

"It's just a blessing to be here, to walk around, and to see my kids," he said.

Robertson missed the final regular-season game in 1999 after the accident, but he returned for the playoffs.

But his luck didn't get a whole lot better. Robertson fractured his lower leg in the AFC Championship Game at Jacksonville and wasn't able to play in Super Bowl XXXIV.

Today, he's the team's director of player development.

THE MUSIC CITY MIRACLE

Kevin Dyson wasn't even supposed to be on the field.

During the final seconds of Tennessee's AFC Wild Card game against the Buffalo Bills on January 8, 2000, he was on the sideline getting ready for at least one more play on offense while Tennessee's return team was taking the field. The Titans had just fallen behind 16-15 on kicker Jeff Christie's 41-yard field goal.

The Titans were desperate. Dyson was huddling with his offensive teammates when a familiar voice called his name.

"I was over there getting my mind right for the last couple of Hail Mary plays, and I heard Coach Fisher call my name, and I thought, 'What's he calling my name for?'" Dyson said.

Confused, he went to Fisher. He wondered if it might be some sort of mistake.

As it turned out, it was Dyson's call into history.

"Home Run Throwback," a kickoff return play, had just been called, and with receiver Derrick Mason out with a concussion and his backup, Anthony Dorsett, out with cramps, coaches quickly decided Dyson was the man for the job. Coach Fisher, in fact, had to explain Dyson's role to him as he went onto the field, and even then things didn't exactly go off as planned.

The play was designed for tight end Frank Wycheck to field Christie's kickoff and then lateral the ball to receiver Isaac Byrd, who would have had the option to pitch the ball to a trailing player.

> ## — TITAN TALK —
>
> "That's a 100-to-1 shot. I'm just thankful to God we got the one time."
>
> —Joe Bowden,
> linebacker

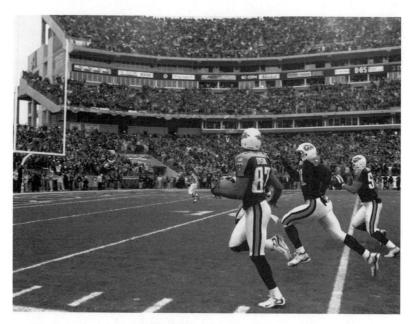

The Music City Miracle.
Donn Jones

Fullback Lorenzo Neal fielded the kick, however, and things went from there. Neal immediately turned around and gave the ball to Wycheck. Things began to unfold as Dyson started running down the field.

"Frank threw it over there, and all of a sudden everything opened up," Neal said. "It was like, 'OK, Kevin, get in field goal range.' And then it's, 'Oh! Forget the field goal. Get a touchdown!'"

And that's exactly what happened. Dyson returned the lateral 75 yards for a touchdown, and after the play held up following a replay review by officials, the Titans were set for a 22-16 victory.

THE INNOVATOR

Titans special teams coach Alan Lowry waited patiently, and nearly 20 years later he finally got his payoff.

It was Lowry's idea to put "Home Run Throwback" in the team's playbook when he was moved from wide receivers coach to special teams coach prior to the start of the 1999 season.

While an assistant coach with the Cowboys in 1982, Lowry saw Southern Methodist University beat Texas Tech 34-27 when return man Bobby Leach took a cross-field lateral on a kickoff and raced 91 yards for a touchdown.

"I had seen it work one time, so you always hope it will work again like that, but there are no guarantees with a play like that," Lowry said. "It's a one-shot deal, and it happened to work."

Many of the Titans admitted in the locker room after the game they hardly even paid attention when the play was practiced. Some weeks, the Titans practiced the play in hotel ballrooms the day before a game.

Dyson was among those who thought the guys regularly involved in the practice version were wasting their time. The colorful carpet and chandeliers seemed more interesting.

"What you have to sell them on is that when we're in a situation like that you have to have a play, and this is our play and we have to execute and make it work," Lowry said. "Now we just have to come up with another one."

MISSING HISTORY

By the time Dyson got home the night of the Music City Miracle, more than 40 messages had already been left on his answering machine.

Presumably, they all saw the play when it happened.

Others can't make the same claim. When Christie's field goal sailed through the uprights to give the Bills the lead, many fans at the Coliseum began heading for the exits and were out of sight by the time Buffalo kicked off.

Many members of the press were in a stairwell leading to ground level when Dyson crossed the goal line. Story has it Cherryn Wycheck was consoling kicker Al Del Greco's wife, Lisa, when her husband, Frank Wycheck, threw the lateral.

At least one other player said his wife missed the play but refused to say it on the record because he didn't want to make her feel even worse.

By now, a million Nashvillians will tell you they were in the stadium that day.

George Plaster, a popular radio personality in Nashville, was there—until the end. He missed the historic play. And it was the second time in less than a decade that he walked out on history. In 1992, Plaster also left the seventh game of the Atlanta Braves-Pittsburgh Pirates NLCS at the top of the ninth with the Braves down 2-0. As a result, one of Nashville's biggest Braves fans missed what happened in the bottom of the ninth, when Francisco Cabrera's single knocked in Sid Bream with the winning run.

In Nashville, Plaster was walking across the nearby Woodland Street Bridge when heard the roar of the crowd—Dyson had just scored.

"I'll never forget it, it sounded like a train, it was so loud," Plaster recalled. "I was like, 'What in the world did I just miss?' And the first thing I thought about was Francisco Cabrera."

Plaster turned around and went back toward the stadium, wanting to catch a peek of the scoreboard. What seemed like an eternity later, there was another roar after the review. It was a touchdown.

"Those people would have loved to have heard what I heard, even though I really didn't see it," he said.

At least he wasn't alone.

Throw Back?

To this day, fans in Buffalo still believe Frank Wycheck's lateral was actually a forward pass.

Heck, there was even controversy about a scientific survey performed by a Rochester, New York, professor who studied whether the pass should have been ruled illegal. Professor Mark Bocko said he told the reporter covering the story that there wasn't enough concrete evidence to decide one way or the other after his analysis; the paper's headline said his findings "offered proof" that the pass was illegal.

So it's a sore subject in Buffalo, to say the least.

Legal or illegal, the Bills fired special teams coach Bruce DeHaven following the season because of the play. Head coach Wade Phillips lasted one more year before he, too, was replaced.

The play remained a bitter memory for Phillips for some time. In the days leading up to Tennessee's season opener at Buffalo the following season, the coach walked onto the practice field pirouetting every 10 feet or so, mimicking the throwing motion of Wycheck on the play.

He referred to the play as "Home Run Throw Forward."

Bills owner Ralph Wilson has called the playoff loss to the Titans more devastating than any of his team's four Super Bowl defeats.

See Ya, Indy

The RCA Dome in Indianapolis was loud on January 16, 2000. So loud that Colts quarterback Peyton Manning was forced to use a silent count on offense. Why, you ask? Because a good number of the

57,097 fans on hand that day weren't cheering for the Colts. They were from Nashville, cheering for the Titans.

What they witnessed was the team taking the next step to the Super Bowl.

The Titans beat the Colts 19-16 in the AFC Divisional playoff game, thanks to the longest touchdown run of running back Eddie George's career, a stifling defense, and some good eyes from a few folks on the sideline.

George's 68-yard touchdown run was big, as it gave Tennessee a 13-9 lead in the third quarter. Defensively, the Titans harassed Manning throughout the game, throwing him off rhythm and forcing him into one incompletion after another.

The biggest emotional swing in the game, however, came after Colts return man Terrence Wilkins returned a punt 87 yards to the Titans three-yard line in the fourth quarter. The Colts were in good position to tie the game at 16-16. The crowd was in their favor.

Not so fast, the Titans said. While standing on the sideline, kicker Al Del Greco and strength and conditioning coach Steve Watterson told coach Jeff Fisher they saw Wilkins step out of bounds right in front of them, at the Indianapolis 35-yard line.

Fisher took their word for it, and the Titans decided to review the play. During the next few minutes the RCA Dome was rocking. Players and coaches on the Tennessee sideline bombarded Del Greco and Watterson with questions about what they'd seen.

Finally, the officials announced they were reversing the call, and the return was brought back.

The Titans held on and advanced to the AFC Championship Game.

LOOK WHO'S DANCING NOW

The Titans swept the season series from the Jaguars in 1999, and a trip to Super Bowl XXXIV was on the line when the teams met in Jacksonville on January, 24, 2000.

The night before the game, Titans coach Jeff Fisher got his players fired up by showing them a clip of Jacksonville's players dancing and singing "Uh Oh, the Jaguars" Super Bowl song. The Titans had somehow gotten their hands on the tape.

"It was very touching to see [former Oiler defensive tackle] Gary Walker singing," Titans quarterback Steve McNair said of the clip. "That was all fun and games. They were all excited. They had reason to be excited, they were playing at home, and they had a great chance of winning.

"But somehow we spoiled that."

Then a riled-up bunch of Titans went out the next day and won the game 33-14 and advanced to Atlanta for Super Bowl XXXIV.

For Walker and the Jaguars, the music came to a screeching halt. Jacksonville's season was over. McNair ran for two touchdowns and threw for another, and Derrick Mason opened the game up with an 80-yard return following a safety.

"This game wasn't lost because of no song, no cockiness," Walker said. "To make a long story short, we just went out there and got our a---- kicked."

SUPER FUN

The week leading up to Super Bowl XXXIV in Atlanta was a new experience for most of the Titans.

All of the hype, the extra large media turnout, and the extreme pressure of the big game—it was enough to send one player down the drain or at least into a drainage pipe.

On the Thursday before the big game, Titans coach Jeff Fisher walked onto the team's practice field at Georgia Tech and found some of his offensive linemen pushing a gigantic drainage pipe around the field.

It wasn't a new conditioning drill. Titans rookie offensive lineman Craig Page, who happened to be an All-American at Tech, was inside.

"Our club is relaxed," Fisher said. "They are poised, and they are enjoying themselves.

"I told them ... if they sensed that any of the coaches were beginning to tighten a little bit, just let me know, I was going to send the coaches home."

TURNING FEISTY

It was Super Bowl week. All for one and one for all, right?
Well, eventually.

As the Titans prepared for the Rams, tension mounted as the game drew closer. By week's end, they were at each other's throats— literally.

In the final drill of the Friday practice inside the Georgia Dome, the first-team defense worked against the first-team offense in a two-minute drill.

Following an incomplete pass down the middle of the field, safety Blaine Bishop and receiver Derrick Mason came to blows. The two were separated but then tried to get at each other again before they were sent off the field for the remainder of the session.

A sign of troubled times? Hardly.

Bishop's mood was never good on Friday, and Mason rarely backs down when he's confronted. So the two of them swinging at each other didn't come as a shock to anyone.

Cooler heads eventually prevailed. They hugged at the end of practice.

A COLD RECEPTION

Chattering teeth. Bulky coats. Gloves. Heaters.

This can't be the Super Bowl, can it?

The Titans certainly didn't mistake Atlanta for San Diego when they arrived in town the week of Super Bowl XXXIV. Some of them made a big mistake by not bringing enough clothes.

"Our guys will have pneumonia by the time it's over with," Titans general manager Floyd Reese said.

Yes, the Titans needed every bit of material they could get their hands on during Super Bowl week, and some of them weren't too happy with Mother Nature. They didn't expect Florida weather, but they didn't count on temperatures being in the 20s during the week with below-zero wind chills because an ice storm hit the city late in the week.

The Titans also didn't like the icy treatment they received at the Super Bowl. Their mandatory media sessions were held in a poorly heated tent adjacent to their hotel during the week, while the Rams were tucked away inside an expansive—and heated—ballroom at their hotel.

The Titans eventually got more heaters in their tents, but that also created a headache. The heaters were so loud coach Jeff Fisher couldn't hear the questions from the media at his press conferences each day.

The temperature didn't heat up much outside. Fortunately, the game was played indoors.

> — TITAN TALK —
>
> "The Rams are inside? See, we're the stepchild, we get no love."
>
> —Mike Jones, defensive lineman

Hey Good Buddy,
How About a Ticket?

Long-lost cousins, old high school buddies, neighbors from years back—you name it, when the Titans made it to the Super Bowl, they all surfaced.

Players, coaches, and team officials were bombarded with ticket requests for the big game in Atlanta. Some were familiar, others weren't.

"A lot of them are saying they went to high school with me, so they're wondering what I can do for them," Titans general manager Floyd Reese said. "The only thing is I went to a high school [Liberty Union in Brentwood, California] that graduated about 150 kids. I know most of those people intimately.

"I never heard of any of these people. It would be different if I went to a high school with 3,000 kids in it or something like that, so that you don't meet everybody. But it's a small town in northern California, everybody knows everybody."

One That Got Away

Starting free safety Marcus Robertson didn't play in Super Bowl XXXIV.

Starting strong safety Blaine Bishop was knocked out in the third quarter.

But somehow in the second half the Titans managed to slow down St. Louis quarterback Kurt Warner and the high-flying Rams offense—until a play called "Nine-Ninety-Nine" blew them out of the water with 1:54 to play. It was Warner's game-winning, 73-yard pass to receiver Isaac Bruce.

The Titans actually had two very good chances to blow the play up, beginning with defensive end Jevon Kearse.

Kearse, who wasn't much of a factor most of the game, got by his man and got to Warner just a second too late. Some contend it was a second too early.

You see, when Kearse hit Warner as he threw the football, it caused the pigskin to sail short. As a result, Bruce had to stop in his tracks and come back for the ball.

If not for that, Titans cornerback Denard Walker might have been able to make a play on the ball. Defensive coordinator Gregg Williams thinks he might have intercepted it.

But as things turned out, Walker stumbled, and he couldn't get around fast enough to make the play. What could have been a huge play for the Titans turned out to be the difference in the game.

And a moment Walker will never forget.

"I was in position and didn't make the play," Walker said. "I hate that it had to end like that especially."

When the team's season was celebrated at a downtown parade a few days later, Walker kept a low profile as players hung out in the Coliseum tunnel at the end of the parade route. A part of him felt guilty. He's quiet by nature, but he was especially quiet that day.

Few blame Walker for allowing the touchdown. Since, there's been more talk about safety Anthony Dorsett taking a bad angle in trying to get to Bruce, which allowed him to take it the distance.

"[Walker] covered Isaac well," Rams coach Dick Vermeil said. "Isaac just went back and got it, the gifted athlete that he is."

ONE LAST DRIVE

Quarterback Joe Montana did it in Super Bowl XXIII for the 49ers. In the closing minutes, he drove his team 92 yards down the field for the game-winning score against the Bengals.

In Super Bowl XXXVI, Patriots quarterback Tom Brady was a hero. He engineered a last-minute drive that produced a game-winning field goal against the Rams.

With the Titans trailing 23-16 in Super Bowl XXXIV after a St. Louis touchdown, quarterback Steve McNair was faced with a huge task himself. It was his chance to be a hero.

Only 1:54 remained on the clock when the Titans got the football at their own 12-yard line. They had one timeout remaining.

McNair ended up putting a drive together that earned him a ton of respect around the league, even if it didn't put the Titans in the end zone.

Back-to-back completions to receiver Derrick Mason and tight end Frank Wycheck moved the ball out to the 28-yard line. A 12-yard run by McNair and a facemask penalty by Rams cornerback Dre Bly on the tackle gave the Titans a first down at the St. Louis 45-yard line with 1:05 remaining.

Titans fans were crossing their fingers and starting to believe.

With 22 seconds remaining, the Titans had the ball at the St. Louis 26-yard line. It was third and five. That's when McNair pulled a Houdini, escaping the grasp of two Rams, including defensive end Kevin Carter, to complete a pass to receiver Kevin Dyson.

"I thought I had him," said Carter, who ended up signing with the Titans prior to the 2001 season. "I had him firmly in my grasp, but his jersey was a little wet and he slipped right out."

The 16-yard completion to Dyson put the ball at the St. Louis 10-yard line with six seconds left. The Titans took their last timeout.

THE LONGEST YARD

For receiver Kevin Dyson and the Tennessee Titans, the moment will always be frozen in time.

Not the Music City Miracle, but the other historic play from the 1999 season. Yes, the play that came up just short. One yard short, to be exact.

With the Titans trailing 23-16 with just six seconds left and the ball on the St. Louis 10-yard line, Dyson ran a slant pattern across the middle and caught a pass from McNair at the five-yard line.

Top: Kevin Dyson reaches for the end zone with the ball as Mike Jones tackles him on the last play of the game during the Super Bowl XXXIV. The Rams defeated the Titans 23-16. Tom Hauck/Getty Images
Bottom: Dyson sinks to his knees in disappointment.
Donn Jones

"When I caught the ball, I thought, 'I'm going to make it,'" Dyson said.

Rams linebacker Mike Jones had other plans, however. He grabbed hold of Dyson's legs and didn't let go.

"I said, 'This time no matter who it is, I can't let him in the end zone. Get him on the ground,'" Jones said. "And that's what I did."

Dyson made an initial surge, and after he was pulled down, he lunged again. He stretched the football out with his right arm, but it was too late. His knee had already touched the artificial turf, which was littered with confetti moments later.

"You can't believe how close it was, but, no, I didn't get in," Dyson said.

Roughly an hour after the game, Dyson stood alone in a corner of the team's locker room at the Georgia Dome, making some final adjustments to his wardrobe. He was remarkably composed, like he had already come to grips with how things ended.

Dyson says he doesn't want the play to be the focus of his career, and he has the Miracle Play to help deflect some of the attention.

Still, the play will forever leave fans in Nashville wondering what might have been ...

"If we get the ball in the end zone and kick the point, there's no doubt in my mind we're going to win the game in overtime," running back Eddie George said. "It was one hell of a ride. We just fell short."

> ── **TITAN TALK** ──
>
> "We put ourselves in position to win the football game when things didn't look so good. One play, one yard. That's what it all came down to."
>
> —Steve McNair,
> quarterback

WHAT HAPPENED?

Safety Blaine Bishop gave his blood, sweat, and tears to the franchise.

He played nine years for the Oilers/Titans, but must live with the fact he missed the biggest half—and play—in the organization's history.

In fact, Bishop wasn't in the Georgia Dome when Rams receiver Isaac Bruce hauled in the game-winning 73-yard touchdown pass from Kurt Warner. He wasn't there when Kevin Dyson was tackled at the one-yard line a few minutes later.

Bishop missed most the second half of the Super Bowl after a collision with Rams tight end Ernie Conwell. He lost feeling in his neck and arms and was taken off the field in a golf cart to Atlanta's Piedmont Hospital for precautionary X-rays. The X-rays turned up negative, and Bishop ended up returning to the Georgia Dome after being diagnosed with a strained neck.

Then he got the bad news.

"Everything was a blur for a while," Bishop said. "They were telling me the score while I was getting X-rays, and I knew we had tied the game at 16-16, but I didn't know [what happened] after that. I ended up finding out the outcome on the way back to the Dome.

"When I came back, everyone was gone and there was confetti all over the ground. When it was over, I felt like I hadn't played in the game."

A NASHVILLE "THANK YOU"

It wasn't the parade they wanted, but it still meant something to the Titans.

Nashville thanks the Titans for an amazing season.
Donn Jones

Two days after their heartbreaking loss to the Rams in Super Bowl XXXIV, the Titans were touched as the city of Nashville celebrated their season.

An estimated 60,000 fans lined Broadway and Second Avenue North, some hanging out of windows and peering down from rooftops.

For more than an hour, fans at the Coliseum sat bundled up in blankets watching a live broadcast of the approaching parade on the scoreboard video screens.

As the parade wound through downtown, Titans coach Jeff Fisher and his players rode in convertibles and were showered in confetti in near-freezing temperatures. Some fans ran up to the cars and slapped high-fives with their favorite players.

And while four of the team's most popular players—running back Eddie George, lineman Bruce Matthews, rookie defensive end Jevon Kearse, and tight end Frank Wycheck—weren't there, having already left for the Pro Bowl in Hawaii, they thanked fans in a recorded message played on the Coliseum's Jumbotron.

"We're going to go back there next year and make sure we win it," Fisher told the crowd before quoting a sign he saw along the parade route: "A setback is just a setup for a comeback."

YOU'RE NO. 1!

The Titans and owner Bud Adams came within one win in 1999 of being able to raise one finger into the air and declare themselves "No. 1."

Just a few months following their Super Bowl defeat to the Rams, Adams held up one finger anyway while making a gesture directed at former Houston mayor Bob Lanier.

It all happened with the cameras rolling. The Titans had gathered to preview the NFL Films highlight video of team's Super Bowl season, and afterward Adams showed off to reporters a Titans AFC championship ring sample.

When asked what he would do if he ever won a Super Bowl ring, Adams pointed at the Houston Oilers AFL championship ring on his right ring finger, then to the sample ring on his left ring finger. Then, with everyone watching, he held up the middle finger on his right hand.

"I'll put it on the middle finger and ask the mayor of Houston to take a look at it," Adams said with a smile.

While it was a bit crude, the comment shouldn't have come as too much of a surprise considering the rocky relationship between Adams and Lanier.

Among other things, Adams was upset with Lanier because he didn't help support a plan for a new stadium to replace the outdated Astrodome. As a result, Adams negotiated a deal to relocate his franchise to Nashville.

One day after his one-finger salute, which was aired on ESPN's *SportsCenter* and on several other national channels, Adams apologized.

"I should not have displayed in public my personal feelings toward the former Houston mayor," Adams said in a statement. "In the future, I will make sure I leave the past behind and concentrate on the great organization and fans we have here in Tennessee."

--- **TITAN TALK** ---

"As usual, Bud Adams has shown a lot of class."

—Bob Lanier,
former Houston mayor

CHAPTER THREE

IT'S GAME TIME

A Big Fiasco

For all the memorable wins following the team's move to Nashville, one memorable loss from the 1998 season stands out—the Chicago fiasco.

It was memorable for all the wrong reasons.

Trailing 23-20 in the final moments against the Chicago Bears, the Tennessee Oilers had a chance to tie the game with a 49-yard field goal.

But when the field goal unit came on the field on a fourth-and-three play, the Oilers were missing one very important player—kicker Al Del Greco. He was nowhere to be found. Del Greco, you see, thought Steve McNair's 13-yard pass to Willie Davis on the previous play was for a first down, and with 21 seconds left there was time to get even closer. So he sprinted to the practice net for a few more swings of his right leg.

"I thought I heard somebody say 'first down.' Obviously it wasn't," an embarrassed Del Greco explained. "I should have known better. I'm the one that screwed up."

Needless to say, things unraveled from there. It looked more like a Three Stooges episode than a three-point attempt.

Punter Craig Hentrich took the field expecting to be the holder, but with Del Greco not out there, he lined up to kick. Backup quarterback Dave Krieg realized the confusion and took the field to hold for Hentrich. When Del Greco caught up with what was going on—it was too late—he tried to get on the field and then tried to get off to avoid a penalty.

Hentrich's kick was blocked, the Bears declined a penalty on the Oilers for having too many players on the field, and the Oilers walked out of Vanderbilt Stadium with a loss, looking a dark shade of red.

Coach Jeff Fisher tried to take the heat off Del Greco by taking the blame for the embarrassing defeat.

"All those things that happened in the last 10 seconds are ultimately my responsibility, and I will take full blame for that," he said. "I've never experienced a loss like that."

> ## — TITAN TALK —
>
> "You can't have the field goal kicker on the sideline picking his nose when he could have tied the game. ... If you are a winning team, you can't let those things happen."
>
> —Bud Adams,
> team owner

FIRE AND ICE

They did most of their work before they were Titans, but safeties Blaine Bishop and Marcus Robertson left their mark on the fans in Nashville nonetheless.

Bishop was the emotional big hitter; Robertson the even-keeled quarterback of the defense.

Bishop was the Fire, Robertson the Ice.

Not many folks expected Bishop to make much of a splash in the NFL. He was a bow-legged five-foot-nine athlete out of Ball State, and he wasn't selected until the eighth round of the 1993 draft.

It didn't take him long to make a big impression on his coaches and teammates. With the Titans, he was a great leader and one heck of an intimidator.

Off the field, reporters knew if they needed Bishop for an interview, they'd better make sure and get him early in the week. The closer it got to game time, the nastier his mood got. Most steered clear of him on Fridays when he was usually foaming at the mouth. On Sundays, he was scary.

Robertson was drafted in 1991 and played with the organization until 2000. He was the communicator on the defense and a playmaker. Robertson recorded 22 interceptions with the team.

Robertson was also a leader in the locker room and on the field.

The two set a good example for some of the team's younger players, especially cornerback Samari Rolle, who grew up watching them operate and eventually joined them. Now he leads the way himself.

— **TITAN TALK** —

"They're like night and day, darkness and light. You have to have that mixture, and we have a great mixture with those two guys."

—Joe Bowden,
linebacker

DEAD CALM

Nothing brings a spirited practice to a screeching halt like an injury, especially to a key player.

Baptist Sports Park has never been quieter than it was on the afternoon of September 20, 2000.

That's the day Titans receiver Kevin Dyson was lost for the season. It was also the start of some bad luck for Dyson in the injury department.

During an 11-on-11 period, Dyson left his feet to go after a deep pass down the middle of the field from quarterback Neil O'Donnell. But when safety Perry Phenix went up with him trying to make a play on the ball, the two collided and Dyson went down.

Dyson's immediate screams let everyone know things weren't good. He stayed on the ground face down for a time before he was helped off the field by trainers Brad Brown and Don Moseley.

Other players approached him to offer encouragement as he left the field, but the news wasn't good. Dyson tore two ligaments in his left knee, and he needed surgery.

In the locker room, some members of the offense began to quietly blame Phenix, suggesting he should have let up. But members of the coaching staff defended Phenix publicly to take the heat off him.

Only Dyson felt worse than Phenix, a normally rowdy guy who kept a lower profile for at least a few days.

ICE AGE

It wasn't Foxboro cold, but it was pretty darn cold on December 17, 2000, in Cleveland, Ohio.

And one of the coldest temperature games in franchise history produced the first shutout in seven seasons, even though not many defensive players stuck around on the field to celebrate after Tennessee's 24-0 win over the Browns.

In fact, it was so cold some players decided to skip warmups before the game.

"Coach Fisher mentioned that was probably the fastest ever a team got back to the locker room after a ballgame," defensive tackle Joe Salave'a said. "But who could blame us?"

Certainly not anyone who was in Cleveland that day, that's for sure. Take it from a sportswriter who showed up with just one glove. It took less than 10 minutes to get from the parking lot to inside Cleveland Browns Stadium. It took more than a half before the bare hand thawed out.

Temperature at kickoff was 20 degrees with a wind chill off Lake Erie of −10. Winds gusted up to 30 miles an hour, and CBS measured the wind chill at the start of the second half as −18. Heavy snow and ice pelted the players throughout, leaving the ground covered.

"Usually when it snows, it's a little bit warmer," running back Eddie George said. "But the combination of snow and a vicious wind chill—it was like a razor blade out there."

George sliced through the middle of the Cleveland defense like a warm knife through butter that day. He switched to longer cleats to get a better grip on the snow-covered field and rushed for 176 yards and three touchdowns. On defense, the Titans held the Browns to just six first downs and 113 total yards for the organization's first shutout in 115 games.

"We went through five gallons of chicken bouillon on the sideline, and there were a lot of guys I didn't recognize in those jackets," Fisher said. "... But I was impressed. We talk about going out there with bare arms and just playing, and we had a lot of guys doing that."

NFL's Best Defense

The Ravens didn't like it, but for that matter, neither did the rest of the NFL.

The Titans rubbed a lot of folks wrong when they finished the 2000 season ranked No. 1 in total defense. To do it, they leap-frogged the Ravens in the final week of the season by holding the Dallas Cowboys to only 95 yards in total offense in a 31-0 victory on *Monday Night Football.*

Without question, it was a heck of a defense. In 2000, the Titans set a franchise record for fewest points allowed in a season (191) and also broke a franchise record set in 1966 for consecutive quarters without a point. The Titans allowed only two touchdowns in the last six games of the season.

"I have never been a part of a defense so dominating," said cornerback Denard Walker, part of a secondary that finished No. 1 versus the pass. "We just want teams to leave here saying, 'Man, those guys are good.'"

The Ravens weren't one of them. Baltimore had a beef with Tennessee's No. 1 ranking, and instead pointed to its own No. 1 ranking in another category—points allowed. Baltimore finished No. 1 in the NFL in that department, allowing just 165 points on the season. The Titans finished No. 2 with 191 points allowed.

"We're the No. 1 defense, there's no doubt about that," Ravens defensive end Michael McCrary said. "The whole country knows who has the best defense."

"Statistically, they finished No. 1, but with less yards," added Ravens defensive tackle Sam Adams. "We gave up less points. You tell me who the better defense is."

The debate was heated in Nashville and Baltimore.

In the end, the Ravens got the last laugh—sort of. In the playoffs, Baltimore beat Tennessee and went on to win Super Bowl XXXV. But in their 24-10 playoff win over the Titans, the Titans held the Ravens to only 134 yards and six first downs. The Titans racked up 317 yards and 23 first downs against Baltimore's defense that day, however.

But yes, the Titans lost.

A CRUEL ENDING

The Titans said it wasn't about his last game, but instead part of a "tough process."

Either way, the ending for long-time kicker Al Del Greco was kind of sad.

The 17-year pro finished his playing career as one of the NFL's most productive kickers. He provided the game-winning kick in the team's first contest at the Coliseum in 1999, a 36-35 win over the Bengals. He kicked 16 game-winners in his career. But unfortunately most Titans fans remember Del Greco most for his dreadful game in the AFC divisional playoff game against Baltimore at the end of the 2000 season.

Del Greco had two of his kicks blocked—one returned for a touchdown—in the team's 24-10 loss, and missed another.

"To have this type of day as a professional ... I never remember missing three in a day," Del Greco said after the game. "I have never thought of that, much less had it happen. I wish I could change it all."

Many fans in Nashville showed no sympathy. In the days that followed fans spoke out with anger, suggesting before television cameras or on talk radio shows that Del Greco should be fired. He became the butt of several cruel jokes.

Then, less than two months later, the Titans released the 38-year-old Del Greco. He never kicked again in the NFL and finished his career connecting on 77.5 percent of his field goals.

Del Greco moved back to Birmingham and for several months refused to publicly discuss his departure from the team—until a Birmingham newspaper caught up with the kicker.

"I think they used me as a scapegoat [for the loss to the Ravens]," he said. "I had three game-winning kicks, and in two games I scored all the points. The problem wasn't the kicker couldn't kick, it was they were not scoring enough touchdowns and relied on the kicker too much.

"I screwed up at an inopportune time, but I think I can still kick."

GOOD DEEDS GO A LONG WAY

Receiver Drew Bennett seemingly came out of nowhere to make the team as a rookie in 2001.

He arrived in training camp as an undrafted free agent from UCLA and as a player who was known in college more as a quarterback than as a receiver.

Few gave him a chance to stick around the NFL long, but Bennett is still going. In fact, he's one of the team's most dependable receivers.

Great route running, smarts, and good hands have had a lot to do with Bennett's success.

Bennett also gives a lot of credit to his younger brother, Richie, and some special phone conversations the two have on nights before games.

Richie, who has cerebral palsy, and Drew call them "karma calls."

"I think my brother is an amazing person," Drew said. "He has an unbelievable personality and good character, and I believe that he has good karma surrounding him. I always ask him to help me out and give me a little karma for the game. I think it helps."

Richie Bennett works hard to build up the karma each week. He does good deeds, which in the past have included everything from buying a homeless person a meal to just helping a lost stranger on campus at the University of California-Berkeley. He has been known to trade dollars for jokes from the less fortunate.

Then each weekend he calls and transfers the positive vibes to Drew. The conversations take place the night before kickoff and are usually brief, two or three minutes.

At home or on the road, Bennett has waited in his hotel room for the calls since his rookie season.

"I'll say, 'You've got my karma working for me?' And he'll say, 'Oh yeah, I've got it working for you—don't worry about a thing,'" Drew said.

It's worked so far. Bennett has caught 89 balls for 1,311 yards and seven touchdowns in his three NFL seasons, and he was awarded a new three-year deal after the 2003 season.

"I am where I am today because of Drew and all my brothers," Richie said. "If I can do anything good for them, I try and do it."

TOUCHED BY TRAGEDY

The entire country was touched by the events of September 11, 2001, the Titans included.

The terrorist attacks on the World Trade Center and the Pentagon took place on a Tuesday, a scheduled day off for the players.

When they returned to practice the following day, many players admitted their minds weren't on football.

Titans quarterback Neil O'Donnell's brothers were in the area of the World Trade Center in New York City and escaped without harm, but he lost friends and acquaintances. Center Gennaro DiNapoli also had friends and a cousin in the World Trade Center. Friends of linebacker Keith Bulluck were also at the Twin Towers that day.

The NFL ended up voting not to play games the following Sunday after first getting input from players across the league. Titans tight end Frank Wycheck said after a conference call with other player representatives the vote was 17-11 in favor of not playing.

Instead of playing the Bengals on Sunday, September 16, some players spent the day supporting blood donors at the American Red Cross in Nashville while others attended church services with their families.

Eddie George proudly carries the red, white, and blue.
Donn Jones

When they eventually returned to action the following week in Jacksonville, many players had a difficult time with their emotions. During the national anthem, Titans defensive end Kevin Carter stood with a hand on his heart, tears running down his cheeks.

Others had to fight to keep tears in as the singing of "America the Beautiful" was shown from New York on the ALLTEL Stadium scoreboard.

It was a time when football didn't seem all that important.

A MONDAY NIGHT NIGHTMARE

The Titans celebrated, and then they were devastated.

Players, coaches, and fans were all in the same boat.

Of all the regular-season losses since the move to Nashville, none was tougher to accept than Tennessee's home loss to the Ravens during the 2001 season. The entire nation watching on *Monday Night Football* got to see one of the more bizarre endings to a football game, one that ended with the Titans losing 16-10.

The Titans thought they'd won it on the last play of the game.

After taking over possession of the football with 3:06 remaining at their own 22-yard line, the Titans quickly drove down the field. On a third-and-goal play at the Ravens' six-yard line with 14 seconds left, quarterback Steve McNair completed a pass to receiver Kevin Dyson, who was stopped at the one-yard line.

With the clock winding down and many of the Ravens attempting to get back on their side of the ball, Titans center Bruce Matthews snapped the ball to McNair, who bowled into the end zone as time expired.

The crowd went bonkers, and kicker Joe Nedney ran on the field to kick the game-winning extra point.

But something wasn't right. Instead of getting ready for the kick, the referees were huddling. And after a lengthy delay the officials called the Ravens for encroachment, ruling Ravens linebacker Peter Boulware made contact with Matthews and guard Benji Olson as he tried to get back on defense. By rule, the play was dead at the time of contact.

With a second chance on an un-timed down, McNair was stopped cold on a quarterback sneak. While the Ravens celebrated, many of the Titans remained on the field face down. Upset fans littered the field with cups and bottles.

"It is very gut-wrenching," tight end Frank Wycheck said. "A sick, sick feeling to watch those guys celebrate when we thought we had won the game."

The Ravens probably couldn't have enjoyed it any more than they did. The loss dropped the Titans to 3-5, and they never recovered. The Titans never got back above .500 and missed the playoffs.

"We're going to drain the Cumberland [River] tomorrow," Ravens tight end Shannon Sharpe said in the victorious locker room. "I'm sure there will be some fans in there, maybe a couple of players, too."

> — **TITAN TALK** —
>
> "It's just a crappy way to lose a game. One minute you are on the top of the world, and think you won the ballgame. The next minute you lose it."
>
> —Brad Hopkins,
> tackle

BORN TO RUN

The Titans saw more than Bengal stripes during a visit to Cincinnati during the 2001 season. In fact, they saw a whole lot more.

With a 20-7 lead and two minutes remaining in the game, the Titans were in the huddle getting ready to punt the football. Then they heard the biggest ovation of the day from the Cincinnati crowd.

It was a streaker, and he was headed right at them after dropping his blue jeans to his ankles.

"It just shocked the hell out of me," Titans cornerback Donald Mitchell said.

> — **TITAN TALK** —
>
> "We turned around and saw this buck-naked guy coming at us. We were like, 'What the hell?' I have heard people talking about wanting to do something like that in college, but I'd never seen anybody do it."
>
> —Aric Morris,
> safety

"[Center] Kevin Long said, 'Watch out, man, they've got an idiot running on the field.' We turned around and next thing I know, the dude had pulled his britches down and was naked. I was like, 'This can't be happening.'"

It was. While security officials chased the man around the field, music on the stadium speakers switched to Bruce Springsteen's "Born to Run." Many of the Titans backed away as he got closer.

Security officials eventually ran the man down.

In the Hot Seat

The entire 2001 season was one to forget for the Titans.

But at least they went out with a bang. Better make that a punch.

One of the most bizarre scenes since the team has moved to Tennessee took place on the sideline of the season-ending loss to the Cincinnati Bengals. That's where teammates DeRon Jenkins and Perry Phenix got into a silly altercation. Punches were thrown, and the two had to be separated. And no one could have guessed why.

Were the two defensive players upset with one another because of a blown coverage? Maybe a misunderstanding on a play call?

No and no.

Instead, the two players were fighting over a seat on a heated bench.

Seriously.

Because the incident took place directly in front of the press box, just about everyone either saw it or heard about it. They saw a couple of rear ends trying to edge the other off the bench. Then they saw Phenix take a swing at Jenkins. Finally, coach Jeff Fisher took Phenix by the arm and pulled him away from the scene after he caught wind of the altercation on his headphones.

Fisher wasn't happy. He told Phenix to cool it. Then Phenix asked Fisher not to make such a scene—that he was "embarrassing" him.

Needless to say, the damage had already been done.

"Guys get upset over different things," Jenkins explained while standing in front of his locker. "It happened. It's nothing really worth getting into detail about. ... It didn't have anything to do with the football game."

After hearing the explanation from Jenkins, reporters headed in Phenix's direction. His explanation was even more amusing—he first tried to act like it didn't even happen.

"I am not talking about it," Phenix said afterward. "Can we talk about the game?"

Game time temperature, by the way, was 37 degrees.

LAYING DOWN THE LAW

They laughed about it all after the game, but before it the Titans were in no joking mood.

Yes, the Titans were 4-6 headed into the December 2, 2001, game against the Browns in Cleveland. They'd lost the week before to the Steelers, and their playoff hopes were flickering at the time.

But to be disrespected by the Browns, a team they'd beaten five times in a row heading into the contest? C'mon.

The Titans claimed it happened, and that's what led to the pregame fight on the field at Cleveland Browns Stadium that day.

It all started during warmups, when the Browns began calling Tennessee's secondary the worst in the league. Some of the Browns told the Titans they were simply a speed bump on their road to the playoffs. They singled out players and cursed at them.

Finally, the Titans decided they'd heard enough.

Titans linebacker Greg Favors, one of the more emotional players on the team, got into a shoving match with Cleveland's Scott Frost in the middle of the field. It was broken up, but when Cleveland's final on-field gathering just prior to kickoff spilled over onto the Titans' side of the field, it was on.

A brawl ensued, and coaches from both teams and some of the game's officials had to separate the players.

"They were talking about how ... we were just in the way for them making the playoffs and stuff like that—you can't do things like that in this league, especially before the game," Favors said.

The Titans ended up winning the game 31-15. They made a statement on the opening kickoff when rookie Dan Alexander caused a fumble with a big hit, and Titans linebacker Keith Bulluck recovered it at the Cleveland 19-yard line.

Five plays later running back Eddie George scored on a one-yard run to give the Titans a 7-0 lead, and the rout was on.

The Browns got the last laugh, however. They beat the Titans 41-38 in the next-to-last game of the season.

> — **TITAN TALK** —
>
> "I guess they thought we were going to come in here and lay down for them. They treated us like we weren't an NFL team. Hey, we haven't been playing like we normally do, but we're still going to fight."
>
> —Josh Evans, defensive tackle

ARCHENEMY NO. 1

It's not uncommon for basketball coaches to hear boo-birds during pregame introductions. Even in 20,000-seat gymnasiums, they're pretty easy to spot.

Head football coaches in the NFL, however, usually go unnoticed. They tend to blend in a little easier, surrounded by overgrown men in mammoth stadiums.

Not Baltimore Ravens coach Brian Billick. Not in Nashville at least.

*There are always fireworks when the Titans
and Baltimore Ravens face off.*
Donn Jones

Over the years Billick has become the most despised opposing coach ever to step foot in the Coliseum. It's also safe to assume Billick and Fisher don't regularly exchange Christmas cards each year.

Prior to the Titans-Ravens AFC divisional playoff game on January 7, 2001, the Titans organization upset Billick by showing his postgame talk to his players after Baltimore's 24-23 regular-season win from a few weeks earlier on the Coliseum's Jumbotron. Holding up a copy of a *Sports Illustrated* that featured the Titans on the cover, Billick made light of the headline, which proclaimed Tennessee was the NFL's top team. Another video clip showed Billick talking confidently about his team's playoff expectations.

The tape was supposed to fire up the home crowd, although many argued afterward it fired up the wrong team.

And after Baltimore's 24-10 playoff win, Billick sounded off on the Titans, calling the scoreboard display a "totally classless" and "shameless" display.

Titans president Jeff Diamond ended up calling Billick to apologize the next day, while also sending notes to two top executives for the Ravens.

NO BOY SCOUTS

Getting a chance to watch the Titans practice up-close is a treat usually available for fans during training camp only, but occasionally other special groups are invited to attend.

When the team entertained a group from a Nashville charity during a minicamp practice in June 2002, some members of the organization ended up feeling a little uneasy. A series of nasty brawls broke out during practice, and some colorful language followed.

Fights on the practice field, of course, aren't all that uncommon. And yes, coaches and players are known to do a little cussing from time to time.

But the fighting was intense and the language was downright vulgar when rookie defensive tackle Albert Haynesworth exchanged punches with offensive linemen Benji Olson and Zach Piller during two separate fights that day. Helmets were ripped off. And did I mention the language?

There were plenty of four-letter words, and we're not talking "Hike!"

It all took place roughly 20 yards away from many women and children in the large group, which was accompanied by members of the team's front office staff. Parents tried to cover the ears of their youngsters, but they weren't fast enough.

When asked how the action might compare to the Mike Tyson-Lennox Lewis heavyweight fight that was scheduled two days later down the road in Memphis, coach Jeff Fisher grinned and replied: "I think just about as many people were watching."

FISH FRY

It was a Saturday in August, the day Jeff Fisher's 2002 team came together.

His players certainly sweated together. Some nearly passed out. Anyone who has stood on the fields at Baptist Sports Park during training camp knows how hot it can get. There's not a single tree to provide shade, and there's usually not much wind, either.

But there was something different about August 3, when the Miami Dolphins were in town for a morning practice and an afternoon scrimmage. The heat was nearly unbearable that day.

A thermometer placed on the concrete registered an unofficial temperature of 133 degrees. On the grass: 114.

The two teams practiced, but they weren't all that productive. Players were irritable, and there were a number of fights. Fisher and Miami coach Dave Wannstedt decided to cut the workout short.

Following the morning session, many of the Titans had trouble mustering up enough strength to even stand up and head for the shower. Fisher remembers most of them being nearly too worn out to even get through a postpractice stretch inside the team's indoor practice facility.

It felt like Miami times two.

"I was talking to the Dolphins players, and they were saying, 'How do you guys do it up here?'" defensive end Jevon Kearse said.

The two teams ended up scrimmaging a few hours later at the Coliseum, but that workout was cut short too because of the extreme heat. Fisher ended up altering the team's practice schedule in the days that followed so the players could recover physically.

At the end of the year he reminded them all of August 3. They'd come a long way.

"Those tough times ... really challenge your determination," Fisher said. "That was certainly an indicative moment."

THE PLANE, BOSS! THE PLANE!

Jeff Fisher said at no time was there any danger.

Some of his players certainly thought otherwise when they looked out the window of their plane in the middle of the night while returning from Minnesota following a preseason game in 2002.

On the runway: dozens of fire engines and emergency personnel. Another red flag: the chartered flight was in Chicago, not Nashville, after an emergency landing. It was supposed to have been a direct flight, but faulty wing flaps on the plane caused it to make the unscheduled stop.

Following a 90-minute delay, players, coaches, and team officials boarded another plane and didn't arrive in Nashville until 5:00 a.m. The players had the day off, so they had an opportunity to make up for lost sleep. The coaches, however, went to work.

"Sleep is overrated," Fisher said. "Forty-five minutes a day is plenty."

STICKING IT TO THEM

Baltimore Ravens coach Brian Billick and the Titans were at it again, this time disagreeing on the meaning of a pregame speech coach Jeff Fisher made to his team leading up to a regular-season game in Baltimore in 2001.

With his team 0-2 at the start of the season, Fisher told his players he didn't care if they dropped to 0-3 as long as they played with a physical edge—as if they brought a "two by four" to the game. Fisher relayed his message to an ESPN reporter the night before the game, but when the reporter relayed the news to a member of the Baltimore media relations staff, Billick ended up catching wind of it and told his players about it prior to kickoff. He threw the two by four into the fire.

Baltimore won the game 26-7, and many of the Ravens said the two-by-four comment gave them all the incentive they needed.

"[The Titans] need to bring a bigger stick next time," Billick said after the game.

Billick's smart aleck response didn't sit well with Fisher or with Titans fans.

Passing Over Randy

Back in 1998, Randy Moss was the most gifted, but also most controversial receiver in the NFL draft.

As everyone knows, the Oilers passed on Moss. But they weren't the only ones—18 other teams skipped over Moss as well.

The Oilers, however, were the only team that took a wide receiver ahead of Moss. They grabbed Utah's Kevin Dyson with the 16th pick while Moss stayed on the board until the Vikings chose 21st.

Throughout his rookie season, Dyson couldn't shake the comparison to Moss, and in some ways it has followed him—and the organization—over the years.

"If [Moss is] there would you take him? We said no, right or wrong. Is it a great decision? Time will tell," Titans general manager Floyd Reese said early during the 1998 season, when Moss started to grab attention with his play. "Ten years down the road we'll see what kind of choice it was.

"But for right now every time Moss catches a touchdown pass, somebody is going to write an article. That's the way it is going to be."

The topic isn't as hot in Nashville nowadays since Dyson is gone, but fans still wonder what might have been.

Dyson was involved in two of the organization's most memorable plays during his five years with the team. His game-winning 75-yard kickoff return for a touchdown in a playoff victory over the Bills and near score on the final play of Super Bowl XXXIV against the Rams both came during the 1999 season.

But so far he hasn't blossomed into an NFL superstar, partly because injuries have slowed him down. Dyson wasn't re-signed by the Titans after his contract expired following the 2002 season, and he signed a one-year deal with the Carolina Panthers. After the 2003 season he signed with the Chargers.

Moss, on the other hand, is a megastar. He has been named to the Pro Bowl five of his first six seasons. He set an NFL record as the only receiver to record 1,000-yard seasons in his first six seasons.

Titans fans will never know what a difference Moss might have made in Nashville. And Moss hasn't spent much time thinking about the Titans passing him over.

"I think when me and Dyson came out in the draft, they said at the time that Dyson was going to be more productive than me. I guess that's just what they felt," Moss said "I guess I just got the last laugh with what I was able to do."

REACHING OUT

Steve McNair and Eddie George have helped the Titans win many football games over the years.

Sometimes their impact reaches far beyond the playing field, however.

Take, for instance, the story of teenager Iran Brown.

During the sniper shootings in the Washington, D.C., area in the fall of 2002, the 13-year-old Brown was shot in the upper left side of his abdomen as he stood outside his Bowie, Maryland, middle school.

Brown's injuries were considered life threatening at the time. He was hospitalized for weeks.

As Brown recovered in the hospital, George sent the boy a personal note and autographed jersey after finding out he was a fan. He did it with little fanfare and didn't want anyone to know about it.

Several weeks later, when the Titans visited Baltimore for a game against the Ravens, McNair arranged to have dinner with the teenager and his family. McNair later arranged to have the boy attend his football camp in Nashville the following summer.

Needless to say, the Titans have a big fan in Brown.

Not in a Buddy-Buddy Mood

He sat through a disappointing loss to Dallas, one week after the Cowboys had lost to the Texans in the expansion team's first game.

Then came a home loss to Cleveland, and a blowout loss at Oakland. When the Titans dropped to 1-4 following a home loss to the Redskins in 2002, Titans owner Bud Adams had seen enough.

And he was pointing fingers.

"I'm very disappointed," said Adams, who left the 31-14 loss to Washington early. "I came in here thinking we were going to get a win, and we didn't look very good. Right now I'm not very happy with what we're putting on the field, and it looks like we're getting out-coached."

Those comments to *The Tennessean* ended up making headlines all over the country. They also created waves at the team complex.

Coaches at practice the following week weren't in a great mood, and Titans coach Jeff Fisher was asked about his owner's outburst at pretty much every conference call with out-of-town reporters the rest of the season.

But Fisher didn't pack up the tent.

"I assure you I'm going to go back to work," he said. "Nobody's quit."

And a funny thing happened after Week 5. The Titans won five straight games and 10 of their last 11 to close out the regular season with an 11-5 mark. They advanced all the way to the AFC Championship Game, where they lost at Oakland.

At season's end, Fisher was given a contract extension. The assistants who had contracts set to expire were given new contracts.

And Adams was again happy. He even patted himself on the back a little bit for giving everyone a jumpstart.

"I'm not one who usually goes public about my concerns with anything," Adams said. "I think when I get to the point where I voice my concerns and let them know, that's something they listen to. It didn't go in one ear and out the other."

THE "OTHER" DYSON

The name was familiar, and for good reason.

When the Titans selected cornerback Andre Dyson with their first selection in the 2001 draft, everyone knew the background. Dyson's older brother, Kevin, of course, was the organization's first pick in 1998, and he became a household name after his involvement in the two of the biggest plays of the 1999 season.

In his first three NFL seasons, Andre Dyson has been consistently good. He ended the 2003 season with 44 consecutive starts, and with 10 interceptions in three years.

But his brother, Kevin, left the Titans after the 2002 season.

"It was fun while it lasted," Andre Dyson said. "We never thought we would play on the same [NFL] team, but once we did we knew it wasn't going to last forever."

ON THE SCENE

"The next Jevon."

That's what some said when the Titans drafted linebacker Keith Bulluck in 2000. Like Kearse, he was expected to go early in the first round, but he dropped much later—all the way to the 30th pick.

And like Kearse, Bulluck vowed to show every team exactly what they missed out on by passing him over.

But unlike Kearse, he didn't get his chance until later.

It was easy to see early on the Titans had something special in Bulluck. On the practice field he made one acrobatic interception after another and was always around the football.

As a rookie, he played on special teams. In his second season, he was ready to start, but the Titans went with veteran Eddie Robinson instead. Former linebackers coach Gunther Cunningham eventually admitted it was a mistake.

In 2002, Bulluck proved to everyone why he should have been playing sooner. He led the team with 180 tackles—the most by a player with the franchise since 1986. In 2003, he totaled 171 tackles and was named to the Pro Bowl for the first time.

Big things are in store for Bulluck, who came out in the same draft class as linebackers Brian Urlacher and LaVar Arrington. The Titans obviously know it, too, because they locked him up to a new long-term deal after the 2003 season.

Bulluck plays with such a high level of energy, the biggest problem he has is calming himself down during the course of a game. It's not unusual to see him running to the locker room just before half-time to get a head start on getting intravenous fluids.

It only seems to give him more energy.

"I think [Keith] is just scratching the surface of what he can really do and he knows that, too," Cunningham said.

REMEMBER THE TITANS

It was almost like a scene out of the movies.

As the Titans held their team meeting the night before their AFC Divisional playoff game on January 11, 2003, against the Pittsburgh Steelers, coach Jeff Fisher dimmed the lights in a meeting room at the team hotel. The players watched an eight- to 10-minute clip from the movie, *Remember the Titans.*

Then the room went quiet when Fisher brought out a special guest after the clip ended. It was Herman Boone, the high school coach who was the inspiration for the movie. In an instant, the room was buzzing. Some players didn't actually believe it was Boone until he started talking. Roughly a dozen players ended up asking him for an autograph.

"He told us we were going to win because we were Titans," defensive tackle John Thornton said. "That kind of gave everybody goose bumps.

"He told us the game was going to be close, we were going to trade scores, and we were going to win at the end."

And that's exactly what happened, with Boone watching on from the sideline.

The Titans beat the Steelers 34-31 in overtime the next night in one of the wildest games ever played at the Coliseum. The winning points came on a 26-yard field goal by kicker Joe Nedney, who got a second chance because of a controversial roughing the kicker penalty on the Steelers.

The made kick also bailed out the person in charge of the fireworks at the stadium, who mistakenly lit up the Nashville sky following the missed kick that was nullified by the penalty.

LOST IN THE BLACK HOLE

Jeff Fisher's plan was working.

The Titans had weathered the early storm by the Raiders in the AFC Championship Game on January 19, 2003, and looked to be in good position just before halftime.

The offense had scored on all three of its first-half possessions, and the defense was holding its own.

It was 17-14 Titans, and they had the football with less than two minutes remaining before intermission. At the start of the second half, the ball would also be theirs. Momentum was on their side as they looked to make it to Super Bowl XXXVII in San Diego.

Then disaster struck. Running back Robert Holcombe was responsible for one fumble, which led to an Oakland touchdown. Then rookie John Simon fumbled the ensuing kickoff, and the Raiders added a field goal. Oakland scored 10 points in just 39 seconds. The Raiders instead took a 24-17 lead into the locker room, and the Titans played catch-up the rest of the way. They never caught up and eventually lost 41-24, putting an end to the 2002 season.

After the game, the locker room at Network Associates Coliseum was like

— **TITAN TALK** —

"We all expected to go to the Super Bowl. We thought this season was going to have a special ending."

—Randall Godfrey,
linebacker

a funeral home. No one felt worse than Holcombe and Simon, who stood in front of their lockers and apologized through the media to their teammates. It was another missed opportunity for the Titans, and the start of a long off season.

PRO BOWL SNUBBING

Good enough to win the AFC South. Good enough to make it to the AFC Championship Game.

But not good enough to have a single player voted into the Pro Bowl?

That's exactly what happened to the Titans during the 2002 season, and the results of the voting left a sour taste in the mouth of many of the players.

No one would have argued if quarterback Steve McNair, linebacker Keith Bulluck, defensive ends Kevin Carter, or safety Lance Schulters had made the Pro Bowl team. They all had solid seasons with stats that placed them among the league's best at their respective positions and were on a team with a 9-5 record when the vote was announced.

But to have not one of them make it was viewed as an insult in every corner of the locker room.

Most players vowed to prove the whole league wrong, and the snubbing became the rallying cry for the rest of the 2002 season.

In the end, the Titans ended up with one Pro Bowler after all. Coach Jeff Fisher took matters into his own hands after he ended up being head coach of the AFC team as a result of his team's defeat in the AFC title game. Allowed to pick one "need" player for the game, he picked Carter, who was a first alternate.

A year later, the Titans finally got some recognition. They were represented by five players at the Pro Bowl—Bulluck, receiver Derrick Mason, punter Craig Hentrich, tackle Brad Hopkins, and McNair, who was the AFC's starting quarterback.

Street Smart

Titans safety Lance Schulters grew up on the streets of Brooklyn.

He used to play tackle football on the pavement. The sewer caps were the goal line, and parked cars were inbounds. At least one game ended when a buddy went through a windshield, Schulters remembered.

On the football field, he's fearless and tough. During his first two seasons with the Titans it wasn't uncommon to see him popping his dislocated shoulder back in place on the sideline, which allowed him to re-enter games. Schulters finally had surgery following the 2003 season to repair the shoulder.

But Schulters wasn't prepared for what happened to him in June 2003.

While leaving a Nashville restaurant during the middle of the day, he was robbed at gunpoint in a parking lot. He used his common sense and not his toughness to get out of that one—he dropped the keys to his black Mercedes and took off running.

"I feared for my life," Schulters said. "Nothing like this ever happened to me in New York City, but it did in Nashville."

Schulters gave police detectives an ID on the suspect. A few weeks later, the 18-year-old turned himself in. For at least a few weeks, Schulters kept a newspaper clipping with a photo of the gunman in his locker as a reminder of what he went through.

Playing for His Mom

Defensive end Kevin Carter is usually one of the first players to show up at the start of training camp each season.

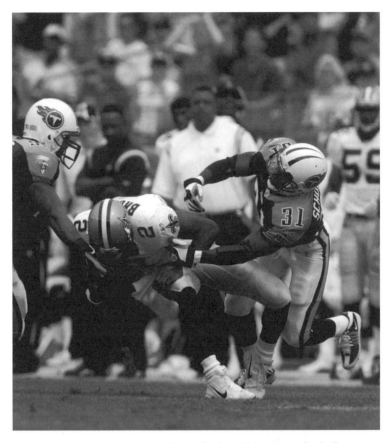

Lance Schulters grew up being fearless while playing football.
Donn Jones

The idea of a fresh start and a new season has always been excit-ing to him.

But when he drove into the parking lot of the Titans facility for the first day of camp in August 2003, his mind wasn't on football. And his heart wasn't in it.

Every year in the past Carter's mother, Virginia, had given him a preseason pep talk. But Carter knew he wouldn't get that boost for his ninth NFL season. His mother passed away on June 25, 2003, following complications from sickle cell anemia. She was 56.

As his teammates passed him by on the way inside to report to camp, Carter sat inside his green Hummer with tears streaming down his face. Then he heard her voice, telling him to pull himself together.

"I had to go function," Carter said. "Life goes on, fortunately and unfortunately. Time can be cruel; it doesn't wait. It certainly didn't wait for me to grieve until I could go start football. It marches on, and you have to try and be strong."

Carter dedicated his 2003 season to his mom, and he also helped raise money for the American Sickle Cell Anemia Association. Carter pledged $500 for each sack during the year. He finished with 5.5 sacks.

A large number of fans and businesses in the Nashville area also contributed in memory of Carter's mom.

"I am my mother's life work. She put everything she had into me and my life," Carter said. "Who I am on the field, off the field, the husband I am, the father I am. That is the silver lining."

KICK IN THE PANTS

Defensive tackle Albert Haynesworth didn't make a good first impression on his new teammates after being drafted in the first round of the 2002 draft.

In minicamps he was involved in several altercations with the team's offensive linemen, and then he showed up late for training camp because of contract issues. He was injured early, and he didn't have a productive first season.

His 2003 season was even more controversial, from beginning to end. It started with another brawl just a few days into training camp. Then, near the end of the year, Haynesworth was suspended for a game by Titans coach Jeff Fisher for another practice field fight, and for conduct detrimental to the team.

A few months later, the coach and player had a disagreement over Haynesworth's off-season workout schedule.

Overall, it's been a rocky first two seasons for the former University of Tennessee star.

Even before his fight with center Justin Hartwig on a 90-degree day in July 2003, Haynesworth was on thin ice with many of his teammates, especially those on the offensive side of the football. When he kicked Hartwig square in the chest during the fight, it not only started a melee, but it put him deeper in the doghouse of the offensive linemen, who were already fed up with his antics and attitude.

Haynesworth blamed it all on the heat, but no one was buying it.

Heat certainly wasn't an issue in December, when Haynesworth was involved in yet another practice field skirmish, this time with offensive lineman Matt Martin. Things escalated to the point Fisher and Haynesworth exchanged words on the field and then later in the coach's office.

Again, it created quite a stir. After practice, some players stood in a hallway at the facility and listened to the play by play of Fisher's tongue-lashing of Haynesworth. Fisher's words could be heard through the wall of his office.

Fisher decided to suspend Haynesworth for the regular-season finale against the Buccaneers, and Haynesworth was told not to even come to the Coliseum that day. He returned and played well in two postseason games.

What's in store for 2004? The Titans have their fingers crossed.

No Stopping Lance

Expressing himself has never been a problem for Titans safety Lance Schulters.

His self-confidence is evident on and off the field. But Schulters was disturbed emotionally during August 2003, when he was forced to make sense of a medical condition he'd never heard of.

After experiencing numbness on the left side of his face, Schulters first wrote it off as a bad tooth. But doctors informed him he had Bell's palsy, a condition that causes the facial muscles to weaken or become paralyzed.

Schulters missed a preseason game and was confused and frustrated.

"I can't really talk right, my face has one part hanging down. My speech is kind of messed up—my words don't come out right," Schulters explained. "I can't cuss as well. Even smiling hurts. But I'm going to deal with it. I have no choice."

Schulters had trouble with his vision for a while, because his left eye kept drying out since it wouldn't completely shut. Eye drops helped, but nothing cured him more than being able to return to the football field.

The NFL cleared Schulters to wear a protective shield during games, but it took him a little while to come to grips with his appearance. While he was recovering, he wouldn't allow television cameras to film him, and he wore sunglasses with his hat pulled down low.

But Schulters refused to let the condition get him too down, and he was in the starting lineup for the season opener. Doctors had warned recovery time could be months.

"Ten days later," Titans coach Jeff Fisher said, "Lance was back on the field."

SAX AND SACKS

Defensive end Kevin Carter has played in plenty of big games and in front of big crowds.

But that didn't keep him from getting a little nervous leading up to a preseason game against the Bills in 2003. After all, it wasn't his reputation as a football player on the line then. On this particular occasion, he was going to be judged for his musical talents.

In the Music City, no less.

While in his game uniform, Carter played the national anthem on his saxophone before the contest, and the performance was carried live on ESPN. The sound delay on the Coliseum's speaker system made it tricky, but Carter received high marks, especially from his surprised teammates.

Not many of them knew Carter began playing the instrument as a pudgy, five-foot-seven high school freshman in Tallahassee, Florida. He played the saxophone in the marching band instead of playing football that year.

Carter also played the national anthem on July 4, 2000, before a St. Louis Cardinals baseball game at Busch Stadium, and he has also performed as a soloist around Nashville during the off seasons.

"My dad had a few of Grover Washington Jr.'s eight-track tapes, and I listened to them when I was a kid," Carter said. "I really liked the way the saxophone sounded, and I wanted to play."

MIDNIGHT STRIKES— AND THEY KEPT PLAYING

Two-hour delays in August aren't uncommon—in baseball. But in football? In Green Bay, Wisconsin? In the preseason?

It happened in Tennessee's 2003 preseason game against the Packers, though not too many folks were happy about it when the game finished the next morning. To be exact, a lightning delay of two hours and 33 minutes resulted in a preseason game that started at 7:00 p.m. ending at 12:46 a.m.

Players from both teams watched TV and played cards in their respective locker rooms during the delay, and some of the Packers surfed the Web since they had access to the Internet. Most of the players expected the game to be called and thought coaches were joking when they eventually told them to stretch. But it was no joke.

Play resumed at 11:01 p.m., and halftime was skipped. One of Tennessee's starters, linebacker Rocky Calmus, was injured after returning to action following the lengthy delay. He admitted he had a hard time loosening up.

The Titans won the game 27-3, but nobody seemed to care afterward.

At the end of the game, only about 10,000 of the 69,126 fans remained in Lambeau Field. Many of those fans chanted "Play ball" after lightning had moved out of the area following a huge storm in the second quarter of the game.

The Titans ended up arriving back in Nashville just after 3:00 a.m. and canceled a light workout so players could catch up on their sleep.

PINCH KICKER

Punter Craig Hentrich usually kicks a few field goals in practice—just in case.

In the 2003 season opener against the Raiders, it paid off. Early in that game, kicker Joe Nedney suffered a season-ending knee injury while assisting on a tackle on a kickoff return. Hentrich replaced him and kicked three field goals from 49, 34, and 33 yards.

Hentrich spent the rest of the season handling kickoff duties as well when the Titans signed veteran Gary Anderson to take Nedney's place.

"I love him," Nedney said of Hentrich. "The guy can come in and do both duties like that with seemingly no problem."

Yes, not bad for a guy who lost in the sectionals of the Punt, Pass, and Kick competition as a five-year-old. Coincidentally, kicking did him in then.

"We used those cheap plastic [kicking] tees," Hentrich explained. "I think the tee went farther than the ball."

STEEL CITY VILLAIN

Titans kicker Joe Nedney might have been acting when he drew a roughing the kicker call against the Steelers in the 2002 playoffs, but the hate mail he received from Pittsburgh was real.

The controversial penalty gave him a second chance to end Pittsburgh's season, and he did just that with the game-winning field goal in Tennessee's AFC Divisional playoff game win.

What Nedney said in his postgame press conference, however, stirred up as much emotion as anything. When asked about Dewayne Washington's hit on him that drew the penalty, Nedney smiled and said, "I think when I am done playing ball, I might try acting."

Pittsburgh's Washington called Nedney's fall to the ground "fake falling."

The Steelers were infuriated with the call, and fans in Pittsburgh were furious with Nedney even though he made a public apology a few days later. When he was injured the next week in the AFC Championship Game at Oakland, some fans wrote him letters to rub it in.

In the 2003 season opener against the Raiders, Nedney suffered a more serious knee injury, one that ended his season. As he sifted through his mail while recovering, he found out folks in Pittsburgh still hadn't forgotten him.

"I opened up one piece of mail and on the paper in bold-faced letters it said: 'Dear Joe, serves you right. You are a [expletive] jerk.' Then it had the guy's name, and 'Pittsburgh Steelers fan.'

"I guess I made my own bed in Pittsburgh. I don't think I'll be vacationing there any time soon."

OLD RELIABLE

He was the little guy with the funny-looking facemask.

That's what many of the Titans thought when they saw 44-year-old Gary Anderson come walking through the door at Baptist Sports Park the first time in September 2003. Some of the rookies were half the kicker's age.

Two kickers, Brett Conway and Neil Rackers, first held tryouts but weren't convincing enough.

Anderson was wading through the Roaring Fork and Frying Pan rivers in Colorado when he got the call from the Titans. He was fly-fishing. In his mind, he had all but retired after 21 seasons.

When the team convinced him to come to town, Anderson first swung by his home in Minneapolis and unscrewed his trademark single-bar facemask from an old Pittsburgh helmet in his basement. The next day he blew the team away with his accuracy. He signed a one-year contract and moved into an upstairs bedroom at the home of punter Craig Hentrich.

But how's this for a kicker?

Near the end of the season, some of the Titans carried Anderson on their shoulders around the locker room in Baltimore chanting his name, "Gary, Gary, Gary!"

It was Anderson's 46-yard field goal with 29 seconds left that ended up beating the Ravens in the playoffs and kept the team's season alive.

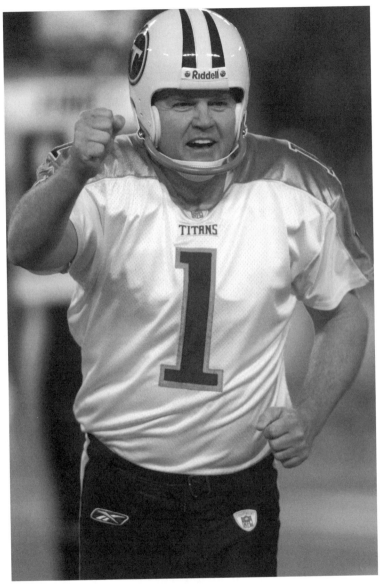

Gary Anderson walked away from his season with the Titans as the NFL's all-time leading scorer, after 22 years of kicking.
Donn Jones

The Titans crossed their fingers when Anderson arrived in Nashville. Their starting kicker, Joe Nedney, was out for the season after one game with a knee injury, and the team needed help.

Anderson ended up making 29 of his 34 kicks with the Titans in 2003. He walked away as the NFL's all-time leading scorer. On his final day, the 22-year veteran also walked away with tears in his eyes.

This time, retirement was for real. But not before he left his mark in yet another NFL locker room.

> ## — TITAN TALK —
>
> "Playing with Gary is an honor. He's a legend."
>
> —Eddie George,
> running back

WHERE'S THE MUSIC?

The Falcons had the Dirty Bird, the Rams had the Bob-n-Weave, and the Redskins had the Fun Bunch.

The Titans didn't have a catchy nickname, but that didn't keep them from getting their groove on in a victory over the Dolphins in 2003. It also didn't keep them from getting fined by the NFL for excessive celebrations.

The players said they were just trying to have a little fun. Cornerback Andre Dyson started the seven-man dance routine when he brushed off his uniform pants as players gathered around him in the end zone and began dancing, moving from side to side. In all, the dance lasted roughly six seconds.

Cornerback Samari Rolle said they had seen the dance on a video by the rapper Chingy.

But in the NFL, a dance party in the end zone has its price.

All seven were fined a total of $45,000 by the league. Defensive tackle Robaire Smith, linebacker Keith Bulluck, Rolle, Dyson, safety Tank Williams, defensive end Kevin Carter, and defensive end Juqua Thomas were all fined either $5,000 or $10,000 for dancing that day. Some of them received their money back through an appeal process.

In the locker room, the emotions were mixed a few days later when the Fed-Ex letters arrived from the league. Some laughed about it while others were ticked off. Some jokingly pointed to others who were also involved in the dance but were not caught by television cameras, and they threatened to turn them in.

"We were just trying to bring some excitement out there," Smith said. "Coach Fisher told us next time to bring it to the sideline."

WELCOME HOME

Titans wide receiver Tyrone Calico learned a lot of things during his rookie season.

Concentrate. Keep your eye on the football. Be consistent.

And, oh yeah, his jersey isn't as valuable as he first thought. Calico, who had four touchdown catches during his first NFL season, returned home from practice one day to find his apartment ransacked. Some cash was missing, and some of his stuff was thrown around the place.

Calico vowed to be more careful about the company he lets inside. But he figured the intruder wasn't a huge fan.

"I was a little insulted they didn't want to take any of my jerseys or anything," Calico said. "They could have racked up."

ANOTHER WARRIOR

When the word *warrior* is mentioned in the same sentence with the Titans, quarterback Steve McNair is usually the first name that comes to mind.

But a quiet, unassuming quarterback by the name of Billy Volek proved he's worthy of the title himself.

Volek showed his mental toughness and ability when he came off the bench to guide the Titans to a 38-31 win at Atlanta on November 23, 2003. He threw for two touchdowns after McNair left the game with a calf injury.

Until then, some outsiders wondered if Volek could do the job, although his teammates had little concern. They saw him take the No. 2 spot over veteran Neil O'Donnell in the preseason.

Certainly no one questioned Volek's ability or toughness a few weeks later when he guided the Titans to a 28-26 victory over the Bills in his first career start. The courageous performance cost him his season, however.

Volek suffered a lacerated spleen and a fractured rib early in the game but played through the pain. He took one big hit after another in the contest, and although he got off the ground slowly on several occasions, he refused to come out.

The next day he was hospitalized, and he was placed on injured reserve when the team re-signed O'Donnell a few days later.

GOOD START, BETTER ENDING

While working in the stock market, Neil O'Donnell has to be able to predict the future to survive.

His time with the Titans, however, proved you can really never know what to expect.

Who could have guessed the popular quarterback would be released twice in a little more than six months?

And who would have thought the team would eventually call on him again after that?

And he'd come back?

Not O'Donnell.

But that's exactly what happened in 2003, O'Donnell's last year as a Titan.

After four productive seasons with the team, including the 1999 season when he went 4-1 as a starter in place of an injured Steve McNair, the team released O'Donnell in February 2003 to get below the NFL's salary cap.

O'Donnell wasn't pleased to say the least, but the Titans promised to re-sign him, and they eventually did.

But at the end of the preseason, the Titans released him again. They again blamed it on finances, but the team was also ready to turn the No. 2 job over to fourth-year quarterback Billy Volek.

At that point, O'Donnell was in need of anger management. But the 37-year-old veteran bit his tongue and put on his driving gloves. He took over additional responsibilities in his children's carpool, and after a few months a part of him figured his NFL career was probably over.

But when Volek was lost late in the season with a lacerated spleen, the Titans called on O'Donnell once again. And for the last time, O'Donnell came back.

"I have two AFC Championship rings. I don't have a Super Bowl ring," O'Donnell explained. "But the one thing, I don't want to look back down the road ... and say, 'I wish I had come back for those last couple of weeks.'"

In the end, O'Donnell didn't get the Super Bowl ring he wanted. But in his 100th career start in the last regular-season game against the Tampa Bay Buccaneers, he went out in style and on his own terms.

With McNair resting for the playoffs, O'Donnell stepped in and passed for 232 yards and two touchdowns in a 33-13 win over the Buccaneers. After the game, he had his picture taken on the field

Neil O'Donnell was released by the Titans twice in six months,
but he came back in style when the Titans needed him.
Donn Jones

at the Coliseum for the first time with his two young sons, Devon and Dylan.

At the end of the season, he also walked away with the respect of the teammates and coaches he came back for. During his 14-year NFL career that also included stops with the Steelers, Jets, and Bengals, O'Donnell also learned the stock market maybe isn't so crazy after all.

DANCE HOME RAY, RAVENS

The Titans danced on the logo in the middle of the field and in the locker room afterward danced some more—Ray Lewis style.

Tennessee's 20-17 AFC Wild Card win over the Ravens on January 4, 2004, did so much more than just advance the Titans in the playoffs.

It finally got the monkey off their backs.

Leading up to the game the Titans had to field one question after another about Baltimore's five-game winning streak in the series. Most of the veterans tried to explain how many of the younger players weren't even around for most of those games during the slide, and history had nothing to do with the upcoming game. But they still felt the pressure.

And after they beat the Ravens that night in Baltimore, they let out plenty of frustration.

Titans receiver Derrick Mason stomped on the mid-

> ## — TITAN TALK —
>
> "From what happened in the locker room after that ballgame, I don't remember this team or any team that I've been associated with, even after the AFC Championship game in Jacksonville [1999 season], as excited as they were."
>
> —Jeff Fisher,
> head coach

field logo and said, "It signified them going home and us beating them up."

He called Baltimore's head coach, Brian Billick "arrogant," along with some of his players. He was upset because many of them left the field without congratulating them.

"After each game we've lost against them, we shake their hands and go about our business," Mason said. "That just goes to show how truly arrogant those guys are."

In the locker room, a handful of players gathered in a circle and did their best impersonation of the dance Lewis does during introductions at Baltimore home games. It was a rowdy atmosphere to say the least.

Freezing Together

Titans offensive line coach Mike Munchak was cold standing on the sideline, but he had to have been mighty proud, too. Somewhere, former Titan lineman Bruce Matthews must have been feeling pretty warm inside himself.

Because on a frigid night in Foxboro, Massachusetts, an old offensive line tradition survived the elements.

When the Titans played the Patriots in the AFC Divisional Round on January 10, 2004, the temperature at kickoff was four degrees. The wind chill was –10. Fans in the stadium were having trouble drinking beer because it kept turning to slush.

It was the coldest game in the history of both franchises.

But the team's starting offensive linemen kept plowing ahead, bare-armed and all. They didn't want to break a tradition started by players before them, Hall of Famers such as Munchak and Matthews.

According to the code of the offensive linemen, whatever a player wears in the regular-season opener, that's what he must wear at the end of the season, too. So if a stocking cap wasn't a part of the September gear, it can't be used in December or January. The same goes for long-sleeved shirts and extra socks. Anyone who breaks the code is fined.

During the game, the starters—tackles Brad Hopkins and Fred Miller, guards Benji Olson and Zach Piller, and center Justin Hartwig—were dressed for summer, even though it felt a lot more like winter. No sleeves, no ski masks.

And while it took them a little longer to thaw out afterward, they said it was worth it.

Barrrrrrely.

ONE THAT GOT AWAY

His teammates forgave him, but Titans receiver Drew Bennett still hasn't forgotten.

Chances are he never will.

On the final drive of Tennessee's 2003 season, in an AFC Divisional playoff contest against the New England Patriots, Bennett made two spectacular catches as the Titans drove down the field in the closing minutes.

But on a fourth-and-12 play from the New England 42-yard line, Bennett was unable to haul in a Steve McNair pass just inside the 15-yard line. The ball bounced off his hands and fell to the ground just after a pair of New England players collided with him.

If Bennett had held on, it would have been a first down, and the Titans would have been well within range for a potential game-tying field goal. With another big play, they might have scored a touchdown and won the game.

Instead, the Patriots held on for a 17-14 win, and they went on to win Super Bowl XXXVIII a few weeks later.

"Guys in the huddle were saying, 'Somebody's got to make a play,'" Bennett recalled. "There I was. That was my chance, and I didn't come through."

McNair once again displayed his leadership by what he did following that play on the Tennessee sideline.

As the final seconds ticked off the clock and the Patriots began celebrating, McNair went over to where Bennett was sitting with his head down and gave him a hug.

He offered words of encouragement, not a finger in blame. If the situation presents itself again, McNair said he wouldn't hesitate to go back to Bennett.

"I have been in a situation like that, coming up a yard short [in Super Bowl XXXIV], and it is always going to stick in your mind, it is always going to be there," McNair said.

"Drew made two fantastic catches everybody's done forgot about to get us down there, but when you drop one, that is what everyone remembers last. Drew is going to relive that, and he is going to play it in his mind over and over again. But the only way you can resolve that is to get back in that same position and make the catch."

It would have been understandable if Bennett had chosen not to make himself available in the locker room after the game. But with reporters surrounding his locker, Bennett stood and answered every single question. He offered no excuses, only apologies to his teammates.

Months later, Bennett still couldn't keep from thinking about the incomplete pass.

"I think about it every time I wake up," he said. "That is by far one of the most coulda, shoulda, woulda situations in my life. I don't dwell on it. I don't sit in my bed and be like, 'Oh man, I can't believe I dropped that.' But it is like, 'Wow, I want to get back to that spot where we're a pass to me from going to the AFC Championship Game.'"

CAN'T SHAKE THE PAST

He was in a different team's uniform, wearing a completely different number.

Former Titans receiver Kevin Dyson was a member of the Carolina Panthers when he showed up at Super Bowl XXXVIII in Houston. But all week leading up to the game against the Patriots, all anyone wanted to ask him about was his old team, the Titans.

And getting tackled one yard short of the end zone as time expired in his last Super Bowl appearance against the St. Louis Rams.

In a 60-minute interview session, Dyson fielded 96 questions related to that play. Some reporters asked him how he felt when Rams linebacker Mike Jones tackled him, which secured the win.

Others asked him if he could have stretched farther, if he ever watches the tape, or if he thought he was in. You name it—Dyson fielded the question.

Dyson remains a good sport about it all. He still keeps a photo of his close call in the Super Bowl in his home, alongside an action shot of the Music City Miracle. He's happy he was a part of history.

"You have to take the good with the bad," he said.

ON THE MAP

Receiver Derrick Mason waited his turn, and now the Titans are being rewarded for his patience.

A fourth-round draft pick in 1997, Mason had trouble working his way on the field much during his first three NFL seasons. Veterans such as Willie Davis and Yancey Thigpen were always ahead of him, and when the team signed free agent Carl Pickens in 2000, it looked like Mason might have to wait even longer.

But Pickens, the former Bengal, turned out to be a bust. He was slowed by injuries and a lack of desire. But that only opened the door for Mason, and he kicked it down.

Mason had his best year as a receiver in 2000 and was also named to the Pro Bowl as a return specialist.

As he enjoyed his time in Hawaii, he made a promise to himself to get back—only next time as a receiver.

In 2003, after his third straight 1,000-yard season, Mason was selected to the Pro Bowl as a receiver.

In was a crowning accomplishment, though Mason is far from satisfied. Now he wants to get back again. No one is doubting him anymore.

"Derrick is a great receiver," quarterback Steve McNair said. "But I always knew he was capable of this."

CHAPTER FOUR

THE COACH

BACK IN THE DAY

When Titans coach Jeff Fisher thinks of Keyshawn Johnson, he doesn't think of the player who coauthored a book called *Just Give Me the Damn Ball!* In it, Johnson talked about his playing days with the New York Jets.

Fisher also doesn't think of the player who the Buccaneers thought they'd be better off without.

Instead, Fisher remembers Johnson as the kid who retrieved a missing moped or as the youngster who was always eager to carry schoolbooks.

While Fisher was playing football at the University of Southern California, Johnson was the eight-year-old who made himself at home in Fisher's apartment.

"My junior year I literally came home, and there was a young man in the kitchen cooking something on the stove," Fisher said. "It was Keyshawn. He was just always around, one of the neighborhood kids that hung around."

Johnson grew up just a few blocks away from the Coliseum in Los Angeles, and he pretty much spent all his free time hanging around the USC players. He got to be especially close with Fisher and some of his roommates, who shared an off-campus apartment.

"One day we had a moped stolen from the apartment," Fisher said. "[Keyshawn] had it back in two hours."

Johnson became a ball boy for USC, and he eventually played there after first playing two years at a junior college. Johnson was a two-time All-America selection at USC, and the Jets made him the No. 1 pick of the draft in 1996.

"When he came out at the combine his senior year, I'll always remember I introduced him to [Titans general manager] Floyd [Reese] and Keyshawn said, 'When your coach was at USC, I used to carry his s- - -,'" Fisher said. "Keyshawn said, 'Now he's going to carry my s- - - around.'"

Fisher and Johnson still talk occasionally. Johnson, in fact, said Fisher has always been a strong mentor of his.

"As a ball boy you get the opportunity to know all of the players. I started to befriend them, and your relationship grows over the years," Johnson said. "Jeff is not the only guy—Bruce Matthews was there, and Ronnie Lott and Marcus Allen. ... Whenever I've ever needed anything from any of those guys, I could pick up the phone and call them. I've been able to learn about life in general—not just football."

BEWARE OF DOG

At first instinct, some might have thought they were missing out on Take Your Dog to Work Day. A head football coach taking his dog to the office? Well, it's not something you see every day.

But sure enough, coach Jeff Fisher showed up at the team's facility back in 1998 with his dog, Madison.

Then Fisher brought the dog to work again the next day and had her inhabiting a patch of grass in the parking lot.

Sure, a dog is a man's best friend but clearly something was up.

As it turned out, Madison happened to be sending out the type of signals that made her very popular with the male dogs at the time.

As Fisher left the house one day, a handful of dogs in his neighborhood were on the street outside, lurking. So to keep her safe, Fisher loaded her up and brought her to work.

He warned folks around the facility to keep their distance.

"She's watching our trailers and cars," a protective Fisher said. "Get too close and she'll rip your leg off."

UNDER THEIR SKIN

Coach Jeff Fisher chooses his words very carefully.

Rarely does he say much to get the opposition riled up unless, of course, the opponent is the Jacksonville Jaguars.

Something about the Jaguars brings out the best—or the worst—in Fisher.

Two days before Tennessee's Super Bowl contest against the Rams, Fisher took this jab at the Jaguars when asked about his team having to play in four different home stadiums during the move from Houston to Memphis to Nashville: "Well, some have said we have had five home stadiums in four years if you would include ALLTEL Stadium in Jacksonville."

It sparked laughter from the crowd of reporters covering the Super Bowl, and it didn't take long for the news to reach Jacksonville, a city still recovering from Tennessee's AFC title game victory there just five days earlier.

A few years later, Fisher took another unprovoked shot at the Jaguars during a press conference leading up to a 2003 regular-season game.

"The big thing for us this week is that we just keep chopping wood," Fisher said with a smirk.

It might sound like innocent coach-speak, and it would have been had Jaguars coach Jack Del Rio not decided to place a stump and an ax in the Jacksonville locker room as a motivational ploy—to "keep choppin' wood"—earlier in the season after a slow start.

As a result, the Jaguars and Del Rio became the subject of national ridicule when punter Chris Hanson accidentally gashed his right leg while using the ax.

So Fisher's words had a purpose. And again, folks in Jacksonville took notice of Fisher's shot.

Leading up to a game against the Jags later in the season, Fisher got involved in a verbal exchange with Jaguars defensive tackle Marcus Stroud.

So be warned: When the Titans play the Jaguars next, Fisher might just say anything.

PLEASE DON'T CALL ME NOW!

Coach Jeff Fisher addresses his football team each year in a meeting on the first night of training camp.

He gives a long talk about what's ahead and what's expected. It's a tone setter for the season.

At the start of the 2000 season, he got one point across loud and clear.

With Fisher watching on, Titans president Jeff Diamond began welcoming the players and wishing them luck. But 30 seconds into Diamond's speech a cell phone rang in the back of the room. An irritated Fisher looked up. Two rings later, the player silenced it. Things got very quiet before Diamond resumed. When he finished, Fisher

Coach Jeff Fisher keeps an eye on his players on and off the field.
Donn Jones

immediately asked defensive coordinator Gregg Williams to get him a permanent marker.

Once again, there was silence, this time for at least a minute.

Then, before Fisher said another word, he made a square on the wall above a trashcan in the room, and delivered this warning:

"I simply said the next phone that goes off in this room, I am going to break it in that square and it is going to drop in the trashcan," Fisher said.

He promised a fine. The only exceptions: if a wife of a player is expecting or someone at home is sick.

The lecture worked. All season, not another cell phone went off in the meeting room. The next season, things also remained ring-free, until the week before the final game of the season.

The Titans were 7-8 and eliminated from the playoffs. All that was left was a rescheduled game against the Bengals. Players were ready to go home.

But there was a meeting the team needed to attend before the last game. Fisher wanted to use some of the time to pay tribute to long-time offensive lineman Bruce Matthews, who was expected to play in his final game. The video department made a special high-light film of Matthews.

As Fisher was leading up to putting in the tape, a cell phone rang. It belonged to assistant video director Mark Preto, who was standing red-faced in the front of the room. The room went dead silent as Preto began to panic. He couldn't find the right button to turn the phone off.

Then Fisher volunteered to help him with it.

With the entire team watching, he took the phone and threw it against the wall. It shattered into a dozen pieces. Fisher had kept his promise.

"Some guys looked around as they were leaving," Fisher said. "They were like, 'Man, he really did it.'"

TIGHTENING THE REINS

As a former NFL player, Titans coach Jeff Fisher can relate to his players.

He knows their concerns. He's aware of the demands of the job. He understands the pressure. And he goes out of his way to make things as smooth as possible.

Ask just about any one of his players and they'll tell you he's a great coach to play for, a "players' coach."

But that doesn't mean he's a softy.

Step out of line, and Fisher will fine you. Disrespect him, and he'll suspend you. Fail to perform, and he'll cut you.

"The players know he means business," quarterback Steve McNair said.

In the aftermath of Tennessee's 7-9 finish in 2001, his first losing season since his second year as a head coach, Fisher changed some things around Baptist Sports Park. He began running a much tighter ship, and the sailing has been smooth ever since. Some might argue things never were rocky.

Fisher is quick to point out the Titans didn't relax their approach in 2001. But he admitted some things were done after that season to re-establish discipline in some areas.

Aside from cell phone privileges being significantly reduced—limited to just the locker room—he cracked down on players taking a nonchalant attitude when they weren't involved in a drill on the practice field. Players were punished for committing personal fouls in games.

Fisher kicked one rookie off the team for having a female in his room the first day of training camp in 2002. He kicked a second player off the team for the same offense near the end of camp.

When safety Joe Walker showed up for a flight in shorts and was spotted at the team hotel in Minneapolis in a tank top, Fisher wasn't happy, especially since he'd informed the players just a day earlier long pants were required and tank tops were a no-no. Walker was released not long after the team arrived back in Nashville.

Yes, Fisher means business. His no-nonsense approach on the practice field is a constant reminder.

Fisher's belief is he doesn't fine players, "they fine themselves."

The same goes for rules.

"You have to look past just ability alone. You have to be able to trust people and count on people when you have rules," Fisher said.

"The rules are all common-sense type things, but when you have them, you have them for a reason.

"I can scream and yell all I want, but if they don't do it themselves, then it has no impact."

METEOROLOGIST JEFF FISHER

He regularly checks the weather radar on his office computer. He has his very own lightning meter, and he's not afraid to use it.

He's also not afraid to move practice indoors even if it's sunny outside. That's because Coach Fisher knows a thing or two about the weather. If he ever gives up coaching, he could probably land a job at the Weather Channel.

Before practices during the summer, Fisher monitors the radar to see if a storm is approaching. He steps onto the practice field, and his lightning meter tells him how far a storm is off and when it's not safe to be outdoors.

Sometimes his players give him a funny look when he tells them to head indoors because a storm is coming. They're even more surprised when they get inside the team's indoor practice facility and hear the thunder just a few minutes later.

A BIG HAIRY DEBATE

As it grew, so did all the talk about it.

The subject: Jeff Fisher's beard.

For at least part of the 2002 season, it seemed the head coach was about the only one in Nashville not discussing it.

Callers on Fisher's weekly radio show inquired about it. Television commentators were giving their opinions on it as well. Many of Fisher's players admitted family members and friends had also been asking about it.

Fisher, usually just a moustache man, had been known to grow a beard during the off season. So he couldn't understand what all the fuss was about when he decided to give it a try during the middle of the season, even though he was making history.

"I can't think of any other head coach with a beard," said Joe Horrigan, who's been with the Hall of Fame for more than 25 years.

In fun, *The Tennessean* newspaper gave its readers a chance to vote on what beard would look best on Fisher, superimposing everything from a "Handlebar and Chin Puff" or "Chin Curtain" or a simple "Goatee" on the coach's face.

Nearly 2,000 readers ended up casting a vote, and Fisher's old look with a moustache won easily.

Fisher ended up keeping the beard for more than two months before shaving it off at the end of the season.

But the talk didn't end then—the beard was back at the end of the 2003 season.

> — **TITAN TALK** —
>
> "I think it's a good look for the wintertime, kind of intimidating. It gives him that rugged lumberjack look if you ask me."
>
> —Henry Ford, defensive tackle

FISHER REUNION

When Titans coach Jeff Fisher went fishing in Belize one off season, he ran into Jeff Fisher. And it wasn't his reflection in the water.

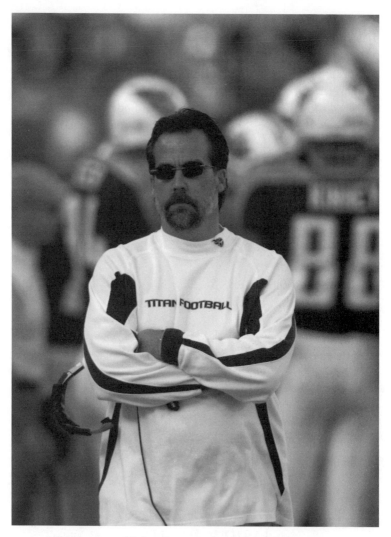

Jeff Fisher sports his beard against the Tampa Bay Buccaneers at the end of the 2003 season. The fashion statement caused a stir in Nashville at the end of the 2002 and 2003 seasons.
Donn Jones

Sound fishy? Well, at the least it was a heck of a coincidence.

The Titans head coach was vacationing with one of his sons in June 2003 when he ran across another guy from Chicago by the name of Jeff Fisher. He happened to also be in the group of six strangers on a fly-fishing trip off the eastern coast of Central America.

Oddly enough, the two had met before. Fisher had signed an autograph for Fisher when he was in his rookie year with the Bears. Coach Fisher spent five seasons with the Bears as a defensive back and return specialist.

"The same name," the coach said. "The only difference was the middle name, and I had more hair."

NICE JOB, STEVE

He's the winningest coach in franchise history, ahead of former head coaches Jack Pardee and Bum Phillips.

And from 1999 to 2003, Jeff Fisher won more games than any other coach in the NFL.

But through it all he still finds himself answering to a different name from time to time: Steve. That's right, Steve Fisher, who coached Michigan to the 1989 NCAA basketball championship.

Jeff Fisher's been called Steve in Nashville, on ESPN, and on countless television broadcasts.

"I was called Steve at the Super Bowl press conference the Friday before the game," Fisher said. "Immediately after I was asked for the 30th time about what it was like to play at four different home venues in four years, have all our difficulties, and then be there and not get any respect.

"The next question was, "Steve, tell me about your defense ..."

At least one of the guilty parties, ESPN's Dan Patrick, said calling Jeff by the wrong name was an honest mistake.

"It wasn't a lack of respect for Jeff, I just wanted to remind people of Steve," he joked.

CHAPTER FIVE

THE FRANCHISE PLAYERS

STEVE McNAIR

ONE TOUGH QB

The stories about quarterback Steve McNair and his toughness are legendary. There's at least one for every year he's been a Titan.

In 1999, he battled back to lead the team to a victory against the Rams just six weeks after having surgery on his lower back.

In 2000, he was held out the entire game against the Steelers because of a sternum injury, but when Neil O'Donnell was knocked out, he entered the game and drove the Titans down the field for a winning score.

In 2001, he stood up for an entire flight because of a painful lower back on a West Coast trip to Oakland but guided the Titans to a win the next night.

In 2002, despite not practicing all week, he took a pain-killing shot before a game against the Giants and finished them off even after the medication had worn off.

In 2003, he dislocated a finger on his throwing hand at Indianapolis, popped it back into place, and re-entered the game. In his mind, a piece of tape on the finger was all he needed.

The list goes on an on, but perhaps McNair's most impressive stretch of toughness came during the 2002 season, when he went an entire month without practicing but still led the Titans to a 5-0 mark.

"If Steve can walk and throw the football," coach Jeff Fisher said, "then he'll be in the huddle."

McNair didn't learn how to be tough overnight. He said it's something he developed growing up on a farm in Mississippi. Or playing against his brothers in the backyard—back then, complaining of an injury was unheard of.

During his nine-year career, McNair has had at least six different surgeries, including one following the 2003 season to remove a cracked bone spur from his left ankle.

"Growing up on a farm, it brings out a lot of mental toughness and physical toughness in you," McNair said. "When the competition level rises, the pain decreases. I just go out and compete.

"You know it is there, but at the same time you have to worry about what's important. Are you worried about this injury? Or are you worried about leading this team to victory?"

— **TITAN TALK** —

"Steve's a warrior. There's not another guy I'd want to go to war with."

—Eddie George,
running back

CALM BEFORE THE STORM

NFL players have all sorts of pregame routines ranging from predictable to bizarre.

Some admit to being superstitious—they'll do the same thing or eat the same food before each game. Some listen to music as they run around on the field in the hours prior to kickoff. Some read *The Bible* or a game program. Others stretch at the same time or location on the field. Some players watch TV.

Titans quarterback Steve McNair sleeps.

McNair's pregame routine is simple: He arrives at the stadium several hours before kickoff, heads out on the field to throw passes and loosen up, and then he heads back into the locker room and finds a quiet spot where he can catch a few Zs.

Sometimes McNair naps in the training room or directly on top of the X-ray table. Other times he'll find a quiet spot in a room away from all of the foot traffic. Once, before a game against the Detroit Lions at the Pontiac Silverdome, McNair slept under his locker, the bottom of which was about two feet off the floor. He put up towels to block the light. Teammates said it looked like he was in a coffin.

When McNair is sleeping, guys steer clear of him. They'd never dream of playing a practical joke on the sleeping quarterback.

"Oh no, guys don't mess with me," McNair said. "They are at the point now where they'll see me walking around and they'll ask, 'Why haven't you taken your nap yet?' They know if I don't get my nap, who knows how I'll play?"

Coach Jeff Fisher said as important as McNair's naps might be, it's just as important to know where he's taking them.

"He has found some pretty unique places," Fisher said. "It's nice to know where he is just in case he oversleeps and we need him."

THE START OF SOMETHING

Since the organization's first game in Tennessee, Steve McNair has been the team's leader at quarterback.

*Quarterback Steve McNair has been the No. 1 guy in
the Titans lineup to lead the team on the field.*
Donn Jones

He started all 16 games the team's first year in Tennessee in 1997, and while injuries have kept him out of some games since, he's been the undisputed man behind center on most Sundays.

In reality, the McNair era began late in the 1996 season. After playing sporadically in 1995 and most of 1996 behind starter Chris Chandler, McNair's big chance came after Chandler sprained an ankle late in the 1996 season. When McNair stepped in and led the Oilers to a December victory, one player finally spoke up and said what many had been thinking.

"You get to a certain point sooner or later you've got to give a guy a chance to do what you drafted him to do," center Mark Stepnoski said of McNair, the team's first-round draft pick in 1995. "I don't see why he shouldn't start. I think he's played well every time he played."

Stepnoski's comments came a day after McNair led the team to a 35-10 victory over the Jets. It only helped fuel the fire on a growing controversy about who the team's starting quarterback should be.

Coach Fisher was in a spot. McNair was itching to start, while Chandler, even with the bum ankle, wasn't ready to hand over the starting spot. Chandler became more irritable just thinking about the possibility. Most players kept quiet.

Fisher ended up naming McNair the team's starter the next week against the Jaguars. He ended up starting two of the team's final three games, including a season-ending victory over Baltimore.

By the end of the season, McNair had convinced just about everyone it was time to officially give him the football for good. And players were willing to step up and say it.

Chandler didn't return for the 1997 season, and McNair hasn't lost his grip on the starting job since.

Chief McNair

The time before practice is usually a time players do some catching up on current events, some last-minute chatting before it's time to get to work.

Others discuss the day ahead.

Before a practice in September 1998, McNair looked at the few moments of peace as a chance to get away.

Rather than joining his teammates for a preliminary stretch or conversation, McNair quietly went over to a place on the field where the running backs typically work on drills. They weren't there yet, so McNair had the location all to himself.

As a few curious onlookers took a peek in his direction, McNair took several long, narrow pads and built them into a teepee. He sat inside, legs crossed, chanting. When folks started to notice, McNair couldn't help but laugh.

"I just had to get some thoughts together, get my mental process together," McNair explained. "I didn't want any attention, that's why I covered myself up, I wanted to be alone, get away from all the guys."

Mississippi Tough Guys

Steve McNair and Brett Favre have taken one course after another at the NFL's school of hard knocks.

It's a good thing they live close enough to carpool—they live in the same Hattiesburg, Mississippi, subdivision.

Over the years, McNair and Favre have earned the reputation for being two of the toughest quarterbacks in the league. They've ignored one injury after another to find a way to get on the football field.

During the off season, the two quarterbacks oftentimes go fishing and hang out. They are good friends.

During the past few years, McNair and Favre have competed against one another twice. Favre guided the Packers to a win over the Titans in snowy Lambeau Field in 1998, but McNair returned the favor during the 2001 season when Favre traveled to Nashville.

McNair still claims to be the better fisherman.

"But [Brett] is a great individual and a great player," McNair said.

> ## — TITAN TALK —
>
> "They are both just regular, good ol' tough guys from Mississippi. They understand they have been given some God-given talents to play football, but it has not gone to their heads."
>
> —Bus Cook,
> both players' agent

FIGHTING THROUGH ADVERSITY

The 1999 season provided one test after another—mentally and physically—for McNair, starting on opening day and ending with the final drive in Super Bowl XXXIV in Atlanta.

There's little question that year helped turn him into the tough-minded leader he is for the Titans today.

McNair was hurt in more ways than one in his first regular-season game in the Coliseum, despite the fact he came off the bench to guide the Titans to a 36-35 victory over the Bengals.

McNair was roundly booed when he limped back on the field with 7:47 left in the contest and his team trailing 35-26. He'd been knocked out earlier with an ankle injury, and most figured his day was done.

But McNair wanted to return and convinced trainers and coaches he could go back out on the field despite the grimace on his face.

McNair ended the day with 341 passing yards and three touchdown passes. His late-game heroics put Al Del Greco in position for a game-winning field goal. But McNair was in no mood to celebrate afterward. He was clearly stung by the treatment.

"It hurt me to see it, but if it worried me, it would worry the whole team," McNair said. "If I'm going to be a leader on this team, if I lay down just because somebody booed me, then the whole team is going to lay down."

A week later, McNair was forced to take a step back. He underwent back surgery to have a ruptured disc in his lower back repaired and ended up missing the next five games. When he returned, he led the team to a 24-21 victory over the previously unbeaten Rams.

But his time away only stirred the fire that started burning not long after the team signed veteran Neil O'Donnell in the off season. Even as the Titans stretched their record to 10-3 in 1999, many still weren't convinced McNair was the right man to lead the team. They pointed to O'Donnell's 4-1 mark while filling in, and when McNair struggled—he didn't throw a touchdown pass in six straight games while throwing seven interceptions over the same stretch—fans on talk radio shows were sounding off. They weren't the only ones.

"A lot of people around the country are wondering why Neil O'Donnell isn't playing, to be honest with you," said former Bengals quarterback Boomer Esiason, with ABC at the time. "... Neil is the perfect quarterback for that type of situation. ... The question is, 'What is [coach] Jeff Fisher thinking about?'"

Fisher never wavered in his support of McNair that year, and in the end, the Titans were rewarded.

It's a Bird! It's a Plane! It's a McNair Fan!

Quarterback Steve McNair hasn't needed to look high and low for fans in recent years.

But when some questioned him early on in the 1999 season, all he had to do was look to the friendly skies one day at practice.

Just a few days after he was booed in the season opener against the Bengals, a small plane flew over the practice field with a message to McNair. The plane was pulling a banner that read: "Fly High Steve—Your Fans." It circled the field as the Titans were preparing to play Cleveland.

The flight was sponsored by Hammock Publishing, a 25-person company based in Nashville. Several employees chipped in on the $300 cost, and the company's chairman, Rex Hammond, matched the contributions to cover the full cost.

The gesture lifted McNair's spirits but also raised a question from inquisitive teammates.

"It showed a lot of class," Fisher said. "The team responded very well to that. They were asking Steve how much it cost him."

> ## — Titan Talk —
>
> "We were somewhat disappointed by the boos, and we wanted to show our support of Steve McNair."
>
> —Rex Hammond,
> chairman,
> Hammock Publishing

New Number?

Steve McNair has worn No. 9 since his rookie season with the Houston Oilers in 1995.

But during the 2000 season he decided to have a little fun with Titans equipment manager Paul "Hoss" Noska. McNair told Noska he was tired of No. 9 and wanted to switch to No. 11 instead. Noska didn't take him seriously at first.

For weeks, however, McNair kept insisting he was sincere, and Noska eventually called the NFL to see if McNair could change numbers during the season.

Then one day McNair walked out on the practice field sporting a new uniform—No. 11. It was Noska's creation, but he didn't provide the jersey with a smile on his face. McNair finally decided it was time for the joke to be over. He informed Noska he wanted his old No. 9 back.

But the quarterback immediately wondered if the prank would be worth it in the long run.

"I got him, but he is probably really mad at me—he was in chaos trying to get me a No. 11," McNair said of Noska.

McNair worried if there might be ramifications down the road.

"I probably won't get a pair of socks this week," he said.

Saving the Day

Ever since the Titans began playing in the Coliseum, the rotation at quarterback, barring injury, had always been the same.

Steve McNair started, and, if needed, Neil O'Donnell relieved him. In 2003, Billy Volek moved into the backup role. But McNair proved one September day in Pittsburgh during the 2000 season that he's certainly capable of providing some off-the-bench heroics himself.

No one thought that would even be possible on September 24. After all, McNair had been knocked out of the previous game against Kansas City with a bruised sternum, and just days before the Pittsburgh game he was still having trouble breathing.

Sure, the running joke with the media each week was always, "There's no way McNair can possibly play on Sunday. The guy hasn't practiced all week."

This particular week, however, the talk was a bit more serious.

But when O'Donnell was knocked to the ground by Steelers linebacker Jason Gildon late in the fourth quarter, it was clear his day was over. His lip was bloodied, and his head was in the clouds.

With the Steelers leading 20-16 with just over two minutes remaining, the crowd in Pittsburgh was roaring, thirsty for more blood as Eddie George helped O'Donnell, a former Steeler, to the sideline.

As things turned out, knocking O'Donnell out of the game was the worst thing the Steelers could have done.

McNair, after spending the first 57:25 of the game on the sideline in a baseball cap, jacket, and headset, grabbed a football, tossed a few warmup passes, and headed to the huddle.

"We had things pretty much in control," Steelers defensive end Kevin Henry said. "Then [McNair] won the game for them."

McNair only threw three passes that day. He completed all three of them, including a 22-yard completion to receiver Chris Sanders on a third-and-11 play—his first throw of the game. A few moments later McNair's 18-yard touchdown pass to tight end Erron Kinney gave the Titans a 24-20 lead and the eventual win. It was another day to remember for McNair.

NEW YORK, NEW YORK

The binoculars from the press box said no. But, once again, Steve McNair said yes.

During his nine-year NFL career, McNair has proven time and again he's willing—and more than capable—of playing in pain.

But what he did on a blustery December day at the Meadowlands during the 2002 season ranks as an all-timer.

Leading up to a game against the Giants, McNair didn't practice all week because of a rib injury and a bad case of turf toe. In fact, he was in so much pain that he didn't throw a football the entire week.

So when he took the field in warmups just prior to the game and was able to throw just a few short tosses, most figured he would be the team's No. 3 quarterback. McNair's first attempt was so painful he was ready to head back to the locker room.

But McNair, as he's done so many times before games, took a pain-killing injection for his ribs. A hole had to be cut in the top of his shoe to make his toe more comfortable.

Then McNair went out and threw for 334 yards and three touchdowns as the Titans rallied to beat the Giants in overtime 32-29.

It wasn't painless. In fact, when McNair crossed the goal line on a two-point conversion to tie the contest late, he had to switch the football from his right hand to his left hand so he could raise it into the air in celebration. The pain-killing shot on the right side had worn off.

"I always want to play," McNair said. "If you're going to be a leader, you have to put it out on the field. I tried to do that."

— **TITAN TALK** —

"I would say he's the toughest guy I've ever been around. I figure if I look up and he's still got two arms and two legs, he's going to find a way to play."

—Zach Piller,
guard

On-Call Nurse

Steve McNair has made plenty of good decisions on the football field—tucking the ball and running when no one's open, finding the right receiver in the secondary, not throwing into double coverage, etc.

But his best decision in life might have come off the field: McNair married a nurse.

As much as McNair has been injured during the course of his NFL career, he certainly needs one.

Mechelle McNair graduated from Nashville's Belmont University in December 2002 with a nursing degree. She didn't have to look long for her first patient—McNair was nursing sore ribs at the time.

She's also dealt with her husband's sore ankles, shoulders, toes, back—you name it.

"She knows a lot more about medical situations than I do," McNair said. "If I have a question or something is hurting, she usually can pinpoint it."

Passing Perfection

When quarterback Steve McNair looks back on his career, his performance against the Texans on October 12, 2003, will surely stand out.

It wasn't the team's biggest win. But to date, it was arguably his best game as a pro.

McNair completed 18 of 27 passes for a career-high 421 yards in a 38-17 win over the Texans. He threw three touchdown passes of 32, 46, and 50 yards to receiver Derrick Mason.

He was so good that afternoon that coach Jeff Fisher thought it was worthy of special recognition.

With less than a minute remaining in the game, the Titans took McNair out of the game during the middle of a drive and replaced him with backup Billy Volek.

On McNair's way off the field, the crowd at the Coliseum gave him a huge ovation.

MVP McNair

Steve McNair had been passed over for awards in the past, so he learned early in his NFL career not to get his hopes up for anything.

Anyone who knows McNair knows he's never really been much of an award guy anyway. All he wants to do is win football games for his team. But when he was named the NFL's co-Most Valuable Player with Indianapolis Colts quarterback Peyton Manning in 2003, McNair was clearly moved.

McNair admitted he ran through MVP scenarios in his head the night before the result was announced. He had come to the conclusion that he probably didn't have a chance because of the two games he'd missed during the season.

But the next day McNair found out he and Manning received 16 votes each.

He got the news from Titans coach Jeff Fisher, who surprised McNair during a team meeting that was called just hours before the Titans departed for Baltimore to play in an AFC Wild Card contest.

With the entire team watching, Fisher opened up an *NFL Record and Fact Book* and began reading off names such as Joe Montana, Brett Favre, and Terry Bradshaw. Then he stopped and lobbed out the question: "Does anyone know what these names have in common?"

After a pause, Fisher gave the answer.

"Well, all these guys won the MVP and won the Super Bowl in the same year," Fisher said with a smile. "So Mac, you have your hands full."

The room erupted. There were handshakes and hugs, along with a few tears.

Later that night, McNair was as emotional as many had ever seen him during his press conference at the team's hotel in Baltimore.

McNair thanked everyone from his teammates and coaches to the front office and training staff, from the voters and Manning to his mom, brother, wife, and kids.

Then he thanked the black quarterbacks who he said opened the doors for him.

"Foremost I would like to thank the guys who paved the way for myself and a lot of other guys, the Warren Moons, the Doug Williamses, the Randall Cunninghams.

"This is something special; this is something I will cherish and take to my grave, that the things I accomplished will help others in the years to come."

McNair was the NFL's top-rated passer in 2003. He completed 62.5 percent of his passes for 3,215 yards and a career-high 24 touchdowns while throwing only seven interceptions, his lowest total since he became the team's starting quarterback in 1997.

THANKS, GUYS

Steve McNair takes care of the guys who take care of him.

After being named co-MVP of the league in 2003, McNair treated his offensive linemen to dinner at Nashville's expensive Palm Restaurant, then surprised them with gifts—Cartier watches and 42-inch plasma televisions.

Starting offensive linemen Brad Hopkins, Fred Miller, Zach Piller, Benji Olson, and Justin Hartwig and backup Jason Mathews all benefited from the quarterback's spending spree.

"He thanked us for the season that we had," said Miller, the starting right tackle. "He thanked us for protecting him and said if it wasn't for us it wouldn't have been possible for him.

"The guy is always giving everyone else credit; he is definitely a team player. That is what makes you want to go out there and fight and give the extra effort for guys like him."

McNair was sacked just 25 times during the 2003 season. The Titans were sixth in the league in sacks allowed.

After the players watched *Rarefied Air*, highlights from the 2003 season on DVD, on a 42-inch plasma TV at the restaurant, McNair told the players they'd all be receiving a TV just like it. At the end of the night, the TVs were loaded into the players' vehicles.

In all, McNair probably spent around $40,000 to $50,000 on the gifts.

"I thanked him several times," said Hartwig, the team's starting center. "Last year was his first Pro Bowl and first MVP so that's quite an accomplishment for him. It was extremely nice of him to hook us up like that."

EDDIE GEORGE

THE BIG HEISMAN DEBATE

Remember that presidential election controversy centering on the "hanging chads" in Florida several years back?

Well, that was nothing compared to the great Heisman debate in Tennessee back in 1997. If you don't believe it, just ask Eddie George. But don't ask him which player he voted for.

During just his second NFL season, George found himself in the middle of a huge controversy in December 1997 by being honest—he admitted he voted for Michigan cornerback Charles Woodson instead of Tennessee quarterback Peyton Manning in the Heisman Trophy race.

That didn't go over well in Tennessee, especially at a time when fans in Middle Tennessee were still Vol crazy and lukewarm about the new NFL team.

UT fans ripped him in *The Tennessean*'s letters to the editor, and he was trashed on radio call-in shows. Some fans threatened to stop going to games and even called George "a traitor."

There was such a stir, in fact, members of the team's front office felt like they had to defend his name.

"I think they would love to have Eddie George as a son, they would love to have Eddie George as a neighbor, they would love to have him as a friend, as anything," general manager Floyd Reese said. "And probably some of those people don't really know him. Whatever he did he certainly didn't intend to make a lot of people mad."

Eventually the controversy died down, but George became a little more reluctant to make his Heisman vote public after that.

THE BEAST

Mention "The Freak" and folks instantly think of Jevon Kearse. The moniker "Air" sometimes splits Steve McNair.

Running back Eddie George went without a nickname during his first few seasons in the NFL, until offensive coordinator Les Steckel pinned "The Beast" on George. It began to stick during the 1999 season, in part because fullback Lorenzo Neal was pushing for it.

"He's a monster," Neal said. "I think that's a good name. I'm 'Beauty,' and he's 'The Beast.'"

GIFT FROM THE BACKFIELD

Some running backs buy their offensive linemen steak dinners. Others hand out Rolexes.

So how did Titans running back Eddie George reward his offensive linemen after his career-best season in 2000? He purchased nine all-terrain vehicles for nine players who helped pave the way. George piled up 1,509 yards on a career-high 403 carries in 2000. He was named to his fourth consecutive Pro Bowl.

The four-wheel Hondas were given to the starting offensive linemen—Brad Hopkins, Bruce Matthews, Kevin Long, Benji Olson, and Fred Miller—along with backup tackle Jason Mathews, backup guard Zach Piller, and tight ends Frank Wycheck and Erron Kinney. The ATVs had a license plate with the player's first name on it. George knew what some might have been thinking, "Hmmm, what would 2,000 yards be worth?"

"I don't know," he said. "If it keeps going, they might want Ferraris."

Running back Eddie George signs memorabilia for Titans fans in the stands.
Donn Jones

MOVE OVER EARL

The walls of Earl Campbell's office are covered with years of memories of great accomplishments.

And certainly the Hall of Fame running back did enough during his career to decorate a mansion.

But something was missing, and when Campbell ran into Titans running back Eddie George at a card show one off season in Houston, he seized the opportunity to collect it.

"I said to Eddie, 'I want to get your jersey man. I don't have anyone's jersey, and I want yours and I want to frame it,'" Campbell said.

George, naturally, was flattered. And clearly taken aback.

"He said, 'Earl, come on man, you know you are one of the greats,'" Campbell recalled. "But I wanted Eddie George's [autographed jersey].

"He seems a lot like myself. I am very impressed with him and his work ethic."

As a youngster, George remembers watching Campbell punish tacklers during his playing days with the franchise. Campbell, inducted into the Pro Football Hall of Fame in 1991, rushed for 8,574 career yards with the Houston Oilers from 1978-1984.

Not long after their meeting, George broke Campbell's all-time rushing record with the franchise.

"[Earl] got to that level by running hard, by his passion to get it done, week in and week out," said George,

> ## — TITAN TALK —
>
> "The biggest thing that impressed me about both of them was that they are both superstars of the NFL, but they never considered themselves in that light and there was always a great hunger to improve and get better. It was a relentless pursuit of bettering themselves."
>
> —Bruce Matthews,
> former Titans center

who toppled Campbell's 8,574 career rushing yards in December 2002 in a game against the New York Giants. "The man put his all into what he did. He played every play like it was his last play. ... To me, it is incredible for me to even be mentioned with him."

REACHING 10,000

Since his rookie year in 1996, running back Eddie George has never paid much attention to personal accomplishments.

But what he did on December 28, 2003, was worthy of recognition.

On that day at the Coliseum, George became just the 17th player in NFL history to eclipse the 10,000-yard rushing mark for his career. When he walked off the field clutching the prized football, quarterback Steve McNair was the first player to congratulate him with a hug. He was swarmed by his teammates.

"I'm just so blessed and honored to be within that group," George said.

George's 78 yards against the Buccaneers improved his career mark to 10,009 yards. What makes his accomplishment even more impressive is the fact that he has never missed a game in his NFL career, which includes 128 regular season starts.

"We saw him be the first back since Jim Brown to gain 10,000 yards without missing a game, which is quite an accomplishment for Eddie," coach Jeff Fisher said.

THE BEAT GOES ON

"When Ray Lewis took the football away from Eddie George, he also took his heart."

*McNair congratulates running back Eddie George on
hitting the 10,000 yards rushing mark in 2003.*
Donn Jones

If that ridiculous theory was uttered once in Nashville and Baltimore, it was uttered a thousand times for three years.

Sure, it might have sounded good, but it was absurd.

Every Titan fan remembers the play that started the buzz: With Tennessee trailing 17-10 against the Ravens in the 2000 season's AFC Divisional playoffs, Steve McNair tossed a ball in the flat to George, who bobbled it, then had it taken away by the Baltimore linebacker. Lewis ended up returning the interception 50 yards for a touchdown, and the Ravens went on to win the game 24-10.

Baltimore ended up winning the Super Bowl a few weeks later. And George ended up having off-season toe surgery. George wasn't the same player in 2001, but it was more because of the surgery than anything else. It forced him to miss most of training camp, and he hardly played in the preseason. George ended up having a career low in rushing in 2001. He later admitted he shouldn't have played in many of the games.

Sure, George hasn't been as productive as he was before that forgettable playoff game, but it's not because Lewis took away his heart. It's partly because the Titans took their run-first approach away from George in 2002, and it's partly because of the wear and tear of eight NFL seasons.

Still, the George-Lewis talk wouldn't go away as the Ravens dominated the series against the Titans over the next few seasons. It picked up steam nationally leading up to Tennessee's playoff game in Baltimore in the 2003 season.

And that night in Baltimore, George squashed the talk once and for all.

George turned in one of his most inspired performances ever in a 20-17 Tennessee victory. He turned 25 carries into 88 yards, doing a good bit of his damage after dislocating his shoulder in the first half of that contest.

George ran right by—and through—Lewis on several runs and never backed down from the intimidating linebacker. At one point he stood toe to toe with Lewis as the two jawed back and forth near the sideline at the end of one play.

Despite the rivalry, George and Lewis have remained friends over the years. They talk on the phone regularly throughout the season and see each other occasionally during the off season.

After the game that night, the look on George's face made it clear he was relieved he'd finally buried the tired subject at M&T Bank Stadium, even though he never came out and said it.

"I could have fed into everything that was being said, how [the Ravens] had my number and Ray was in my head," George said. "But I chose not to. I just chose to focus on the fact that this was an opportunity to go out and battle for something far greater than my personal pride."

BRUCE MATTHEWS

40 ESIER THAN 39

Offensive lineman Bruce Matthews celebrated his 40th birthday on the practice field on August 8, 2000.

First, a large group of players serenaded Matthews with a rendition of "Happy Birthday." Then, as Matthews was leaving the field, his fellow offensive linemen, Brad Hopkins and Kevin Long, doused him with Gatorade.

"Old Geezer," "Grandpa," "Pops," is what Matthews said his teammates had been calling him all day.

"But as long as they don't call me late to the meal, that's fine."

In some ways, Matthews got off easy at birthday No. 40, at least when compared to his birthday trick from the year before.

On his 39th birthday, Matthews was greeted with the same song, but he was also the recipient of a whipped cream pie in the face, courtesy of Hopkins.

Matthews laughed off the pie in the face, but he clearly wasn't thrilled with where it took place—on the practice field.

And by his tone that day, he wasn't kidding.

"[Strength and conditioning coach] Steve Watterson instigated the pie in the face, and he brought me along with the understanding you step on the practice field and that's time to work," Matthews said. "So if we don't win the Super Bowl, I know who to point the finger at."

NICE TRY

Bruce Matthews saw just about everything during his NFL career.

He pretty much did it all, too, and that includes getting penalized for tripping. But he almost made it through his career without getting caught. He was called for tripping the first time in an early season game in 2000—his 18th season. Then he got caught again, sort of, later that year in a game against the Steelers when he threw his leg out in an attempt to slow down a defender.

"I tried to trip," Matthews admitted. "I told the official, 'Is it a trip if you try to trip him and miss?' ... I kicked my leg out, I don't deny that."

OOPS! ... THEY DID IT AGAIN!

Anyone who didn't know better might have thought Bruce Matthews was obsessed. Not with football, but with worldwide teen icon Britney Spears.

Seriously? Well, during his final training camp with the team, all the signs were there.

Pictures of Spears could regularly be found in the 40-year-old's locker, and that's not counting the poster that hung above it one day.

Sure, it was out of character, but perhaps it was his way of fitting in with his younger teammates, or maybe his kids—he had two teenagers at the time.

Truth be told, Matthews isn't a big fan at all. He never has been. He was simply the victim of a prank pulled by his fellow offensive linemen.

By the time it ended, Matthews was embarrassed, upset, and had some explaining to do at home.

It all started over breakfast one morning when the linemen ran across a revealing photo of Spears in *USA Today*. As they passed the paper around, Matthews got a disgusted look on his face.

"What do you want to look at that smut for?" he said.

He didn't let up. At the same time, the wheels began to spin in the heads of fellow linemen Fred Miller, Jason Mathews, and Benji Olson. They'd hit a nerve.

After breakfast, they collected all of the papers at Baptist Sports Park and began putting the photos of Spears in Bruce's locker. When Matthews ripped one picture down, another one would be in its place the next day.

As each day passed, the more upset Matthews got. He began watching his locker more closely. He searched for the culprits. And it became more fun for his teammates.

Then the trio decided to turn things up a notch. They sent the rookies out to buy copies of *Teen Beat* magazine, where they found even more photos of Spears and a poster.

They cut out 40 to 50 pictures of Spears and put them everywhere imaginable—on his hat, in his playbook, on his sunglasses, and even on the bottom of his boots. They hung the poster over his locker.

Matthews eventually exploded, and the trio finally called it quits. The joke was over.

Or so they thought.

A few days later, Matthews kicked his boots off at home. One of his six children raised a very interesting question: "Dad, why do you have a picture of Britney Spears on the bottom of your boot?"

And he thought protecting a quarterback was tough.

THE IRON MAN

If Cal Ripken's known as baseball's "Iron Man," then Bruce Matthews has to qualify as the NFL's version.

During his 19-year NFL career, Matthews played in more games than any full-time positional player in league history (296).

He started every game from November 29, 1987, until he retired at the end of the 2001 season.

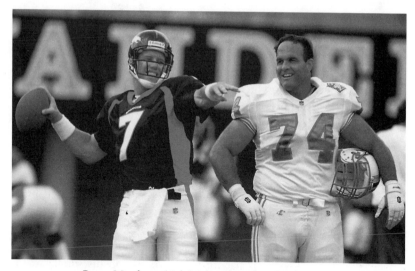

Bruce Matthews (right) jokes around with John Elway
before the Tennessee Oilers-Denver Broncos game.
Donn Jones

He was blessed with good health and a body that was able to withstand the grind of the NFL year after year after year.

Matthews, who played every position on the offensive line during his career, was selected by the Houston Oilers in the 1983 draft. He was named to 14 Pro Bowls.

Over the years he blocked for 15 different quarterbacks and 28 different running backs.

One of his proudest days came during the 2000 season. On a snowy day in Cleveland, Matthews played in his 279th game. It was one more than his brother, Clay, who played 19 seasons as a linebacker with the Browns and Falcons.

The two brothers were honored on the field for a coin toss just prior to the game.

"I think neither [Bruce] or I have a lot of love for those type of ceremonies," Clay said. "Just line up and play."

And that's exactly what Bruce Matthews did. On December 8, 2002, the Titans welcomed Matthews back to town for another ceremony.

The team retired his jersey No. 74 at halftime of a game against the Colts.

"I came to the Oilers, and at my first press conference they held up 74," Matthews recalled with a smile. "I said, 'Man, that's a big slug number.'

"I grew into it over the years."

And he wore it well.

FAREWELL BRUCE

Offensive lineman Bruce Matthews ran off the field with mud caked on his left elbow and holding his helmet high above his head with his right hand.

It ended up being the last time Matthews left a football field in uniform. On January 6, 2002, Matthews played in his last game with the Titans. He ended up retiring six months later.

Just as he did throughout his 19-year career, Matthews kept a low profile leading up to the last game. Even though he knew it would probably be his swan song, he never said so.

But many folks used the day to honor Matthews anyway.

Music he selected was played on the public address system during warmups. Matthews posed for pictures with his family on the field before the game, against the Cincinnati Bengals. Matthews was the final player introduced as the Titans took the field.

Even his high school coach, Dick Salter, made the trip to Nashville to see the game. It was the first time he'd seen Matthews play in person since his prep days.

Matthews was in on just four plays, but he went out with a bang. His final offensive play was a 41-yard touchdown pass from Steve McNair to Derrick Mason.

"I thought, 'If that is my last play, then that's a pretty good way to go out.'"

LIFE WITHOUT BRUCE

Things weren't the same after Bruce Matthews retired, on the field and in the locker room.

Despite being the oldest of the offensive linemen, Matthews was the biggest jokester of them all. Not long after his retirement, he said the thing he missed most about playing was being able to act like a teenager and "be commended for it."

Matthews always had plenty of tricks up his sleeve.

When the Oilers moved to Nashville in 1997 and held training camp at Tennessee State, several players rented golf carts to get around campus and save their tired legs. Matthews was the guy who would rig them up so they wouldn't run, or he'd hide them.

Matthews also created a variety of games designed to keep things fun on the practice field or in the locker room. He was usually the architect of the human pyramids the linemen would make before practices. He was always a fierce competitor in the one-handed grab game, where players took turns tossing a football back and forth using only one hand.

"Bucket ball" was played in the locker room as players tried to toss a football into a laundry cart at the end of the room. Matthews was always the quarterback during Saturday practices, when offensive linemen would run pass routes.

When he retired after 19 years, most of the shenanigans went with him.

"I think everyone has a little Bruce in him," tackle Fred Miller said. "Bruce brought so many things that you just can't put your finger on one particular area. It was the whole attitude and atmosphere."

— TITAN TALK —

"Whenever anything funny was up, Bruce was in the background smiling. He was the instigator."

—Jeff Fisher,
head coach

SAMARI ROLLE

SOCKED TO HIM

Jeff Fisher warned him not to wear them not once, but twice, maybe even three times.

But time and again, cornerback Samari Rolle defied him. Rolle's defense: There's some kind of magic in the socks.

Any Titan fan who has seen them on the cornerback knows exactly what the socks in question look like. They have alternating blue and black stripes that run from his shoes to just below his knees.

"That's the last time you'll ever see those socks," Fisher said after the second time Rolle wore them on the practice field. "I think they are a holdover from his high school play, *The Wizard of Oz*."

But the threats didn't bother Rolle, who was outfitted in the socks on at least one other occasion. He even wore them under his uniform socks on a game day during the 1999 season. They're not pretty, but they're apparently effective.

"These are the socks that put me in position to start. It was the best I was ever playing," Rolle said. "I saw them when Randy Moss went to Marshall—he wore white and black ones. He told me where to get them."

THAT'S MY BOY!

Titans cornerback Samari Rolle has shared a running joke with his mother ever since he started playing in the NFL.

Rolle knows if he makes a big play, chances are his mom, Grace Rolle, didn't see it. Since his high school days, she's been too nervous to watch his games.

"He says, 'Did you see so and so?' Then he says, 'That's right, you didn't see it,'" said Grace, a school teacher at Nautilus Middle School in Miami. "I'll tell him, 'I saw the replay.'"

Grace Rolle still remembers exactly where she was during one of the biggest plays of her son's career. It came in the final minute of Tennessee's 20-19 win over Jacksonville during the 1999 season. Grace Rolle was in the ladies room at ALLTELL Stadium in Jacksonville.

There, she was protected from the pouring rain but blocked out from everything else. So she had no idea her son had secured Tennessee's win by intercepting a pass from Jaguars quarterback Mark Brunell in the end zone with just 57 seconds left.

"I figured if I hear the crowd roaring, I'll know Jacksonville scored the touchdown, but all of a sudden people started walking in the bathroom and I didn't hear any noise, like clapping and cheering or anything," Grace remembered.

Grace decided to find out what happened and so she questioned a rain-soaked Jaguars fan.

"Do you know what happened? Who won?" Grace asked.

The woman looked at her and said, "I don't know if you know this player, but he just intercepted the ball for Tennessee."

"Who was it?"

She said, "Some guy named Samari Rolle."

Grace jumped up and said, "Do I know him? Yes, I know him, he's my son."

She left the bathroom and watched Samari celebrating on the field by doing the Tomahawk chop for Florida State. But it didn't take long for Grace to realize it was safer in the bathroom.

As she watched, she told the guy standing next to her, "I can't believe they pulled it out."

He looked at her and growled, "That s- - - isn't funny."

And all of this happened on Grace Rolle's birthday. As a present, she received the game ball—a gift from her son.

MAKING THEM MISS

The shortest distance between two points is a straight line.

But on a Monday night in Washington, D.C., Titans cornerback Samari Rolle proved it's not the only way to get from Point A to Point B. On that night, getting in the end zone in a hurry didn't really matter, just as long as he got in. And fortunately for the Titans, Rolle did just that.

With the Titans leading 13-7 against the Redskins on October 20, 2000, Washington had the ball at the Titans' 34-yard line with just 10 seconds remaining in the half. Redskins quarterback Brad Johnson wanted to make something happen in the closing seconds, but what happened next turned out to be one of the most spectacular interception returns in franchise history.

Rolle stepped in front of Redskins receiver Irving Fryar to pick off Johnson's pass downfield and then swerved his way through one Washington player after another on the way to the end zone. The interception return totaled 81 yards in all, although Rolle probably ran twice that distance.

And for Rolle, it was all or nothing—the clock read 00:00 well before he crossed the goal line. If he'd been tackled at the one-yard line, no one would have cared.

The Titans won the game 27-21, thanks in large part to Rolle's big play. It was the sixth longest interception return in franchise history.

GOING ALL OUT

Birthdays at Baptist Sports Park are usually better if no one knows about them. Or better yet, if they fall during the off season.

Cornerback Samari Rolle had no such luck on August 10, 2001. And, for that matter, neither did U.S. Senator Fred Thompson just nine days later.

Of all the birthday pranks performed at the team's training facility over the years, Rolle's probably took the cake. The funny thing is he knew it was coming. He just didn't know what, and he was in no position to stop it.

As Rolle exited the doors of the team's indoor practice facility that day, dozens of his teammates armed with everything from whipped cream to cake frosting to pies from the cafeteria were outside waiting for him. Hidden from Rolle's view was a manmade cage that would soon be his temporary home.

Before a suspicious Rolle walked out, he armed himself with a bottle of Pepto-Bismol and a bottle of baby powder.

"It was all I could find," he explained. "I had some other stuff, but Eddie George wrestled them away."

The players grabbed Rolle and threw him in the cage, covering him from head to toe. He remained in the cage for several minutes until someone felt sorry for him and let him out. His photo ran in the newspaper the next day. Titans coach Jeff Fisher suspected Rolle got a "special" treatment because he had not practiced during the first 10 days of camp because of a hip injury.

Then there was Thompson, who stopped by to watch the Titans practice during training camp. He certainly wasn't expecting a pie in the face, but someone in his traveling party slipped up and told a team official it was his birthday, and the attack was on.

When it was over, Thompson, a Titans fan, was a good sport. He said he felt lucky. He had seen Rolle's birthday treatment on the local news just days earlier.

"I felt sorry for that guy," Thompson said of Rolle. "At least they didn't put me in the cage. ... I should have known better than to come out here on my birthday."

— **TITAN TALK** —

"Birthdays are special occasions, but when it's a birthday for someone who hasn't practiced in three weeks, it takes on more significance."

—Jeff Fisher,
head coach

*Cornerback Samari Rolle is tough on the field, but as a Titan he had
to be even tougher to withstand his birthday present from the team.*
Donn Jones

OUT OF SIGHT, NOT OUT OF MIND

When cornerback Samari Rolle left town less than two weeks before the start of the 2001 regular season, upset because of his contract situation, some of his teammates couldn't help but chuckle a bit.

Defensive end Jevon Kearse even wore Rolle's No. 21 jersey onto the practice field his first day away. Safety Blaine Bishop had sported Rolle's uniform the day before, when Rolle was considering leaving town.

Titans coach Jeff Fisher and general manager Floyd Reese, at the same time, were seething. It was a classic case of players versus management. Most of the players were on Rolle's side despite the fact many fans felt Rolle had abandoned the team.

The Titans weren't sure how to react.

"For a player to leave camp is a giant issue," Reese said. "It's not, 'My wife is having a baby, and I am going to miss practice.' To leave camp is probably distasteful to players, coaches, GMs, everyone."

Rolle left town at the advice of his agents. They were dissatisfied with the progress of talks on a long-term deal for Rolle, a member of the Pro Bowl team the year before, who had reluctantly agreed to sign a one-year tender just prior to the start of camp.

When Rolle returned three days later, he made the rounds, apologizing to Fisher, Reese, and his teammates. He was fined $15,000—$5,000 for each day he missed. But in the end he got the long-term deal he wanted and over the years has proven to be well worth the investment.

But he sure created one of the biggest stirs in the process.

"I know because of this some people are going to be on my case every time something bad happens," Rolle said. "... But I can deal with it."

GET A LIFE, COACH!

Samari Rolle is regarded as the team's best video game player, but don't tell that to former Jaguars coach Tom Coughlin. He doesn't want to hear it.

Actually, Coughlin probably wouldn't care these days since he's with the Giants. But he sure didn't like it a few years back when he found out his star running back, Fred Taylor, spent a Saturday afternoon at Rolle's house in Nashville playing video games. The Jags and Titans were scheduled to play the next day.

"I'm surprised at that," Coughlin said. "That's not what I expect [my players] to do when they arrive at a site of an away game, and I didn't know about that. You'd like people to be resting in preparation for the game."

Taylor caught some grief from his head coach, while Rolle found the whole thing amusing. Rolle has been friends with Taylor since the two were in high school, and they've remained good buddies.

Coughlin's words set off a mini-controversy in Jacksonville, while the Titans found his demands ridiculous.

"You are a grown man, no one can tell you you can't go this place and you can't go that place," Rolle said. "As long as you are not missing curfews or anything like that it should be fine."

JEVON KEARSE

NICE IMPRESSION

Everyone had heard stories, though few had seen him in person.

They only knew defensive end Jevon Kearse didn't get his nickname, "The Freak," for nothing.

During a minicamp in Kearse's rookie season in 1999, his coaches and teammates began finding more clues. And that was after he stretched his arms out to show his 86-inch wingspan.

While taking part in a conditioning test conducted by the team, Kearse stunned anyone who happened to be standing nearby in the team's training facility one morning.

When he reported to the vertical jump station in the weight room, Kearse looked around the room and surveyed his surroundings.

Then he popped a question that made everyone wonder what might come next.

"He asked how high the ceiling was, and it was 12 feet," coach Jeff Fisher recalled. "He asked the coach there if anyone thought he could touch it."

Kearse was informed if he could touch the ceiling, he could leave. The test would be over. Kearse did it once and then did it again for anyone who might have missed it.

Later, he turned mundane drills into something worth watching.

Defensive line coach Jim Washburn set up a drill hoping to spark his group one afternoon. Five linemen faced a five-man blocking sled and at Washburn's command, hit it. Then they did some running in place before Washburn sent them on a scramble through tackling dummies and blocking pads before picking up cones placed 20, 25, and 30 yards down the field. The competition to get a cone was fierce.

*Jevon Kearse's (No. 90) physical ability is what attracted the Titans
to him and explains why his nickname is "The Freak."*
Donn Jones

Washburn turned things up a notch when it was the rookie's turn. He challenged Kearse by putting him in competition with four other players. Then he loudly bet Kearse would come up empty handed in the final run.

Kearse surged ahead of the pack and got all three.

"I don't know if I saw what I saw," a stunned Washburn said. "That's the most shocking thing I've seen on a football field."

— TITAN TALK —

"That's why they call him 'The Freak.'"

—Josh Evans,
defensive tackle

"THE FREAK" VERSUS RUNYAN

Training camp was just a few days old in 1999 and already folks were talking about it.

Practice observers marveled at Jevon Kearse's speed during his first few training camp practices as a rookie. His trek to the quarterback looked almost effortless.

But most had been watching tackle Jon Runyan swat away defensive linemen like flies for years.

How would Kearse do against Runyan once they strapped on the pads?

School was in session the first day the two put on pads, and the six-foot-seven, 320-pound Runyan had his way with Kearse. Several times Kearse was pushed around, something that left him visibly frustrated.

"He's got the biggest reach of anyone I ever played against, but he knows what to do with it, too," Kearse said. "In college you just use your speed and run around the corner and get the quarterback. Here I'm going to need some more game."

Runyan seemed to get great enjoyment out of silencing the rookie.

Over the course of the season the two players didn't necessarily become great friends, but they made each other better. Kearse was named NFL Defensive Rookie of the Year, and Runyan had an outstanding season as well, his last year with the Titans.

But the two would one day meet again, only this time not on the practice field. It was the 2000 season, and Runyan was in his first year with the Eagles. It was apparent they had not missed each other too much.

The meeting was hardly a friendly competition.

"I talked to him during the game to tell him how dirty he was," Kearse said after Tennessee's 15-13 victory over the Eagles. "He was grabbing me ... and there were a couple of cheap shots. ... [But] I think I rose to the challenge and out-tussled him."

Now, they're together again as members of the Philadelphia Eagles.

GATOR HATERS?

And Jevon Kearse thought they were happy because he played for the Titans.

Even before his first NFL game Kearse was being praised and made over by fans all over Nashville, but he thought something was strange. Many of them were wearing orange and white, with the word "Volunteers" or the initials "UT" on their shirts and hats. Some were sporting black and gold and the words "Commodores" or "Vandy."

Kearse had previously always been booed in Knoxville—the Vols and Gators hate each other. And Vandy fans don't care much for the Gators either. Kearse played at Florida, of course.

Finally, he figured it out.

"Every Vol fan I see says, 'I'm glad you left Florida a year early,'" Kearse said. "I guess they got tired of me coming through there and hitting the Tennessee and Vanderbilt quarterbacks."

A "FREAK"-ISH BEGINNING

Jevon Kearse was a safety and later a college linebacker at the University of Florida. When he elected to leave school after his junior season, most figured he'd go early in the first round.

But to the delight of the Titans, Kearse lasted all the way to pick No. 16. The Titans grabbed him and felt fortunate.

During the second half of the 1999 season, they began to realize exactly what they had.

"I thought he'd be productive, and I expected him to make a lot of plays as a rookie but not this many," coach Jeff Fisher said.

Kearse burst onto the scene as a rookie, and his performance stands as one of the most dominant by a defensive lineman in league history. He led the AFC and set the NFL single-season rookie record for sacks with 14.5, and he also led the NFL with 10 forced fumbles.

He was named NFL Defensive Rookie of the Year by the Associated Press and was named to the first of three consecutive Pro Bowls.

"I wanted to show all the teams that passed me up ... that they missed out, and I think I did a pretty good job of starting that," Kearse said.

Kearse earned 49 of the 50 first-place votes for the Defensive Player of the Year award with the stray vote going to Redskins cornerback Champ Bailey.

Kearse seemed almost embarrassed the day he was announced the winner. His teammates chanted his name as he entered the locker room, and his locker was surrounded by a herd of reporters and cameramen.

The mob scene was a regular occurrence during Kearse's first year. His former locker mate, defensive tackle John Thornton, used to joke he wanted to change lockers because he never had enough room because of the big crowd.

Barely hours after his rookie season ended, some, including Kearse, were already wondering what Kearse might do for an encore.

"I'm thinking," Kearse said. "Aww, how am I going to top this?"

SHUTTING UP SHAR

Jevon Kearse had already dominated plenty of veteran tackles during his rookie season. By late December, he'd been named to the Pro Bowl and was a popular subject with national writers.

"The Freak" was pretty much a household nickname.

But Steelers right tackle Shar Pourdanesh wasn't impressed. And he mistakenly riled up Kearse leading up to the final regular season game of the 1999 season.

"Jevon? Who's that?" Pourdanesh joked with reporters in Pittsburgh. "I'm not scared of anybody in this league, especially a rookie. ... OK, if Mike Tyson lined up, I might be scared. I'm going to get [Kearse]. C'mon, he's a young guy. Some hand grenades in the jockstrap and he'll be done."

Kearse had not been disrespected as a pro until then. Heading into that game, he'd already totaled 13.5 sacks and nine forced fumbles. When he got to Pittsburgh, Kearse ripped a photo of Pourdanesh out of the game program and hung it in his locker before the game. Then he blew past Pourdanesh during the contest, stripped Steelers quarterback Mike Tomczak, picked up the football, and took it in for a touchdown.

During the game, several Titans had confrontations with Pourdanesh. Safety Blaine Bishop went after him because he said Pourdanesh intentionally poked him in the eye, and Kearse had to be restrained on several occasions.

"You can't talk like that and then not back it up," Kearse said. "He's a real dirty player. He stuck his finger in my throat one time under the pile, and I know he did some other stuff. I guess the game showed who should have been talking and shouldn't have been."

BAD HAIR DAY

Hair one day, gone the next.

But for Titans defensive end Jevon Kearse, there apparently was a good reason to go bald during the early portion of the 2001 season.

"Did you see [Jevon's] last haircut?" teammate Samari Rolle asked out loud. "He had no choice but to cut it all off after that."

To some degree, Kearse admitted that was true. Kearse has never been known to wear his hair long, but some of his teammates did a double-take when he decided to break out the razors on his own hair one day and go bald.

Kearse said he was pretty much left with no choice.

"That is the risk you take when you go from barber to barber," Kearse explained. "You get your hair cut different ways."

KEARSE SEES KEARSE

From his second-row seat behind the Titans bench, Joseph Kearse Jr. watched his younger brother run onto the field before a jam-packed crowd at the Coliseum one chilly November day in 2001.

He heard more than 67,000 fans cheering for "The Freak," a regular occurrence at the stadium, and had a chance to join in on the noise.

By then, defensive end Jevon Kearse had already hit the big time.

The moment was special for the brothers. It marked the first time Joseph was able to watch Jevon play football live since he was a high school safety back in Fort Myers, Florida.

That's because Joseph Kearse spent from July 25, 1996, until November 1, 2001, locked up at the Desoto Correctional Institution in Arcadia, Florida. He was incarcerated for robbery with a firearm and armed burglary.

Kearse invited his brother to Nashville for the Thanksgiving Day weekend game against the Steelers.

Kearse estimated he visited his brother twice each off season during the jail term, even though his visits created some major buzz.

But Joseph didn't even get to watch his little brother play in Super Bowl XXXIV on television because a New Year's Day fight left him in disciplinary confinement. A warden said it wouldn't have been fair to let Kearse watch and not let others in the isolated section just because he had a brother in the game.

Jevon Kearse said if his brother had chosen a different path in his early life he might have ended up in the NFL himself. Joseph Kearse was regarded as a top-notch receiver.

"He had more potential than me," Jevon said. "His talent was just a given, where I probably had to work a little more."

A ROADBLOCK AND DETOUR

Jevon Kearse's first three NFL seasons had been almost a breeze.

But one giant leap and awkward landing in the 2002 opener against the Eagles set him back nearly an entire season, and he hasn't caught up since. It eventually led to the Titans letting him walk away after the 2003 season.

As Kearse chased down Eagles running back Dorsey Levens on the second play of the 2002 season, he leapt to avoid teammate Henry Ford. When he landed, he fractured the fifth metatarsal in his left foot.

The crowd at the Coliseum went silent as a cart took Kearse off the field. By halftime, word had leaked out Kearse's injury was serious.

Kearse had surgery the following week, but his recovery took him longer than originally expected. When he did return 13 games later, he wasn't the same player. He ended up playing just four games on the season and had just two sacks.

Kearse's mood was sour that entire year, and his foot didn't give him much reason to smile. He snapped at reporters and tuned others out. He ended up having a second surgery less than a month after the season.

"[The 2002 season] wasn't fun," Kearse said. "It was pretty tough inside. Besides being aggravated, I was feeling like it was a punishment for something I did.

"At first I was miserable and hating myself. I didn't want to communicate with my friends and family. Pretty much the only communication I wanted to have was with my teammates, because those are the guys I feel connected with."

Kearse's 2003 season got off to a better start, but an ankle sprain again kept him from returning to his old form. He finished the year with 9.5 sacks but didn't register a sack in his last seven games. Time and again he had to leave the field limping.

When the Titans were faced with a decision on whether to place the franchise tag on him in February 2004, which would have allowed them to keep him one more season, they opted to let him go. Then, on the first day of free agency, the Eagles signed him to a long-term deal. The days of "The Freak" in Nashville were officially over.

DRAWING A CROWD

As a member of the Titans, defensive end Jevon Kearse couldn't walk down a street in Nashville without getting recognized. It's safe to assume he's now dealing with the same thing on the streets of Philadelphia as an Eagle.

But when Kearse took a trip overseas during the summer of 2003, he was doing a pretty good job of keeping a low profile.

He was just another tall guy in Amsterdam, probably mistaken for a basketball player more than anything. He ended up navigating London with few interruptions as well.

But as Kearse and a friend walked through a courtyard in Prague, he suddenly became "The Freak" again. A young voice called out his name and blew his cover.

In an instant Kearse was surrounded by high school kids from Vermont. Tourists from everywhere then converged on him for autographs and pictures.

"I have been to plenty of Titans games, and he has drawn crowds, but this was unbelievable," said Jeff Rubin, a close friend of Kearse. "Once people knew who he was, whether they were from Hong Kong or Canada or any part of Europe, they just wanted to touch him. It created a circus atmosphere."

Kearse isn't nice to quarterbacks, and he doesn't necessarily care for the media, but to his credit he has a good way with people on the streets. He signed autographs for an hour, and by the end of the day he ran into actor Matt Damon. Damon proclaimed himself a big fan and invited Kearse back to his place for drinks and conversation. The two talked about everything from filmmaking to football.

But Kearse had already given plenty of others something to talk about that day.

FRANK WYCHECK

A GREAT PRO

Frank Wycheck was an unheralded tight end when he arrived in the NFL in 1993.

He was a sixth-round pick by the Washington Redskins, who ended up releasing him just two years later.

It turned out to be the best thing that could have happened to Wycheck—and the Titans.

Wycheck retired from the NFL following the 2003 season, bringing an end to the career of one of the city's most popular and successful players.

Wycheck's 505 career receptions rank fourth all-time among tight ends behind Shannon Sharpe (815), Ozzie Newsome (662), and Kellen Winslow (541). He was named to the Pro Bowl three times.

During his time in the league, however, he also left his mark on those around him.

The tight end's blue-collar approach earned him respect from teammates and the competition. He was a stand-up guy in the locker room who was always available for interviews, win or lose. His down-to-earth personality also made him a fan favorite the day the Oilers moved to town.

Wycheck played in 137 games with the Titans and caught 28 touchdowns. During one stretch he had a team-record 99 consecutive games in which he caught at least one pass.

But the signature play of his career ended up being a lateral on a kickoff return. It was Wycheck who threw the cross-field pass to Kevin Dyson during the AFC Wild Card game against the Bills on January 8, 2000. Dyson then went 75 yards for a touchdown in Tennessee's win.

"That's something I'll never forget as long as I live," Wycheck said.

*Frank Wycheck digs in after catching the ball for
extra yardage against the Buffalo Bills.*
Donn Jones

At the age of 32, Wycheck was hesitant about announcing his retirement, but a number of concussions weighed heavily into his decision. But he hardly left with regrets.

"I did everything I set out to do and much more," Wycheck said. "From a guy who wasn't even supposed to be in a training camp, let alone to where I ended up, I'm truly proud and I couldn't ask for anything more. It's been a truly great ride."

— TITAN TALK —

"When we moved to Nashville, Frank was the first one off the bus. He hit the ground running. He led the parade."

—Jeff Fisher,
head coach

CHAPTER SIX

ALL ACCESS

Back Off Barber!

Since the team's days in Houston, every year during training camp the veterans have had a field day on the heads of the rookie class. They break out the razors and shave some gruesome patterns into the noggins of the first-year players.

Over the years the offensive linemen have generally been the most creative. In training camp 2002, just over a month after long-time offensive lineman Bruce Matthews announced his retirement, the linemen paid him a tribute when they butchered rookie lineman Kyle Benn's hair. All that was left when they finished Benn's hairdo was a shaggy No. 74 on the back of his head.

In 2003, offensive lineman Marico Portis had a face shaved into the back of his head. A cigarette fit perfectly in between the folds of skin where the mouth was located.

Usually, every position group has fun with the clippers—and the rookies.

The hair art of the Titan linemen is unique.
Donn Jones

But in 1997, the team's first season in Tennessee, one Oiler didn't go for it.

Oiler Brent Burnstein, a six-foot-seven, 288-pound undrafted rookie free agent out of Arizona State, was known for his long hair. Teammates called him names like "Howard Stern" and "Fabio" because he wore his dark hair all the way down to the middle of his back. And he was proud of it.

So proud, in fact, Burnstein left camp when he caught wind of the head-shaving ritual. He didn't give the defensive linemen a chance to get their hands on his locks.

"I have seen players leave camp for a lot of different reasons, but I've never had one leave because he didn't want his hair cut," Titans coach Jeff Fisher said. "Obviously his hair was more important to him than his football career."

THE LONGEST MILES

Almost like clockwork, Titans general manager Floyd Reese heads out the door each day for his afternoon jog.

Only Mother Nature gets in his way, and she has to be acting pretty ugly to do it. Pounding the pavement helps Reese clear his mind.

Reese had plenty to think about one birthday several years ago. His thoughts were focused on: "How in the world am I going to get all these bugs off of me?"

Reese, even as one of the club's top executives, isn't immune to the horseplay—or foul play—that goes on when someone has a birthday.

One afternoon, Reese was on his way out the door for a jog when Titans coach Jeff Fisher called him into a room full of players. Once there, Reese was "treated" to a rocky rendition of "Happy Birthday" by the rookie class.

What the unsuspecting Reese didn't realize was while the rookies were singing, some veterans were sneaking up on him from behind. They grabbed him, held him down in a chair, and covered him with whipped cream from head to toe.

Some say he looked like a smaller version of the Stay-Puft Marshmallow Man from the 1980s movie, *Ghostbusters*. Determined not to let the episode throw off his routine—and not wanting to take the extra time to shower—Reese quickly cleaned himself off with towels and took off for his jog, wearing the whipped cream-stained clothes.

It was a run he'll never forget. The sugary smell attracted everything in his path.

That episode apparently made a lasting impression on Reese, born on August 8, 1948.

"Our general manager won't attend practice on his birthday any more," Fisher said. "He's worried about getting a pie in the face or something else happening."

> — TITAN TALK —
>
> "I was so sticky, and bugs and flies were following me every step of the way. I'd run through the gnats, and the gnats would just stick to me. It took me forever to get all that stuff off of me."
>
> —Floyd Reese,
> general manager

SPREADING SOME SUN

Defensive end Kenny Holmes was drafted in the first round of the 1997 draft to sack the quarterback.

Some of his defensive line teammates had other things in mind, though.

As a rookie, Holmes was the guy placed in charge of getting sunflower seeds for his teammates. He quickly discovered they make the seeds in sour cream and ranch flavor, along with the regular.

"They can put some sunflower seeds down, that adds up," Holmes said of his fellow defensive linemen. "You'll see me carrying a big book bag sometimes to meetings, that's what's in there."

Holmes was smart. He bought a case of seeds early on. He ended up doling out about six giant bags a day.

"I'll be happy when I get a chance to put that off on somebody else next year," he said.

DOES THIS REALLY WORK?

Some kickers, from the very beginning, are suspicious.

After all, not many of them had ever done the pelvic thrust as a stretching exercise. They certainly had never hopped around on their tippy-toes like some kind of ballet dancer in practice.

But when they take a peek back and see veterans such as kicker Joe Nedney and punter Craig Hentrich doing the same thing, they figure it must be for real.

A few days later they find out the embarrassing truth.

The kicker ballet is a regular part of training camp every year, and at least one unsuspecting kicker always falls for it.

Here's the deal: Each summer, Titans strength and conditioning coach Steve Watterson lines all the kickers in a row, with the rookie stationed in the front and the veterans behind him. The vets, of course, know the drill.

With a video camera rolling high above, Watterson then puts the kickers through a series of wacky and borderline obscene stretching exercises.

They skip, jump in the air, try and find something on the ground while blindfolded, move a football from one butt cheek to the other. You name it—they do it. They're told it's to help with balance.

The whole thing stays a secret until a few days later, when, put to music, it's shown in front of the whole team at a meeting.

"We had one player where after it was done he said, 'That was the best workout that I've ever had. Can I get a copy of that? I want to bring it back to my college,'" Watterson said. "Little did he know three days later we play it for the whole team."

CODE RED

Rookies should respect the veterans. Don't lie to your teammates. Follow tradition, as silly as it might seem at times.

If you're a new Titan and you follow those simple rules, you should be safe.

Any player who doesn't, however, stands the chance of being humiliated like John Henry Mills, Mike Leach, Aaron Koch, and the list goes on and on.

All three were victims of a dreaded Code Red. They're not alone.

Each year dozens of new players walk through the doors of Baptist Sports Park. Someone ought to show each and every one of them a photo of Mills, who bucked tradition one day back in Houston and as a result nearly ended up buck-naked—all because of some skimpy donuts.

As tradition has it, rookie players get donuts for the veteran players on Saturday mornings. Mills was running late one morning, so he took the easy way out and bought two bags of Hostess mini-donuts. Needless to say, his teammates weren't impressed. They certainly weren't full after eating them.

The next week, Mills fumbled again on his assignment. Eventually, he quit trying.

He ended up paying for it.

His teammates stripped him down to his jock strap and tied him to the gate in front of the team's facility. When the gate went open, Mills went with it, and players told him "Hello" and "Goodbye" as they passed by.

Coach Jeff Fisher isn't a big fan of hazing, but when the team moved from Houston to Nashville a Code Red remained a hush-hush option for veterans looking to set a difficult youngster straight.

Players handle the administration of the Code Reds, but they first must get permission, starting with strength and conditioning coach Steve Watterson. He then takes the proposed mission up the chain of command, where it is either approved or disapproved.

When Leach, a tight end, made the poor choice of informing some rookies about a longstanding Thanksgiving prank—then fibbing about it when confronted—he was tied to a stick and dipped into an ice tub over and over. Eventually, the truth came out. He didn't—he was left in the ice tub for quite a while.

When Koch, a guard, refused to carry the helmets of his teammates during training camp in 2000, the offensive linemen taped him to a goalpost and covered him with everything from Pepto-Bismol to Aqua Velva to powder.

Unfortunately for Koch, it was the day his wife and mother-in-law attended practice for the first time.

He should have known better.

MIKE MUNCHAK DAY

Titans offensive line coach Mike Munchak is in the Pro Football Hall of Fame. His uniform No. 63 was retired by the organization, and he was named to the inaugural class of the Titans/Oilers Hall of Fame.

He's been with the team since 1982, either as a player or a coach. Some jokingly call him the "favorite son" in the building.

But even Munchak's not safe from being the butt of a joke.

During a team function a few years back, Munchak was praised by a high-ranking member of the organization and pointed to as an example of how to do things.

"If everyone would just work as hard and dedicate themselves like Mike Munchak, then ..."

Before the sentence was over, the wheels were spinning in the head of Titans strength and conditioning coach Steve Watterson.

The next day, "Mike Munchak Day" pamphlets were all over the walls at Baptist Sports Park. They read:

"Let it be known from this day forth, every second Friday of March will be a corporate holiday in honor of our Columbia Blue Blooded Idol, Mike Munchak.

"From Metro Center to the Stadium shores of the Cumberland River;

"From the Hallowed Halls on Post Oak in Houston to his future shrine in Canton;

"Let not a single Titan/Oiler voice be still for we shall all sing, Hail to Mike Munchak."

Then, the final line: "In order to be exempt from work on this day you must commit to one hour of personal reflection about how you can better serve the Titans as much as Mike Munchak."

Everyone got a kick out of it, including Munchak.

THE KNUCKLER DID IT

Punter Craig Hentrich might have trouble throwing a knuckleball, but he can sure punt one.

Just ask some of the NFL's top return men, who've been battling the fluttering ball for years. You can even ask Titans special teams coach Alan Lowry for that matter.

Not long after the veteran punter arrived in Tennessee, Lowry saw Hentrich practicing this so-called knuckleball punt. Hentrich's believed to be the first in the league to perfect such a boot.

But Lowry wasn't intimidated—until he tried to catch one.

"I really hurt my thumb," Lowry said. "Let's put it this way: I don't catch them anymore. I always thought I could catch any punt, but not that punt. But we've had several people have that happen to them."

Hentrich's teammate, Derrick Mason, doesn't waste his time trying.

"Nope, I won't catch it," Mason said. "I don't have to play against him, so it is not my duty to catch a knuckleball."

Punter Craig Hentrich punts his signature knuckleball.
Donn Jones

Hentrich began working on the hard-to-handle punt in the tricky winds of Green Bay not long after entering the league in 1993. He drops the ball a different way on the knuckleball than he does on a routine punt, and the way he makes contact with the pigskin takes the spin off the ball.

After a while, some players around the league began to figure Hentrich out—they stayed away from the knuckleball, too. But many brave ones have tried over the years and failed. Take return man Dennis Northcutt, for instance. He muffed Hentrich's knuckleball during the 2002 season when he was with the Cleveland Browns.

"It was like throwing a leaf up in the air and trying to catch it," Northcutt said. "A kicker that can do that is awesome. That kick was a knuckleball!"

At least he recognized it.

AS THE TITANS TURN

Every year during training camp there are tremendous battles on the practice field.

Then there are the battles for the remote control when it's time for the midday soap operas.

Every year the roster changes, but since the Titans have been in Nashville, the team has always had its share of die-hard soap opera fans. Other players like to give those guys grief, hiding the remote from time to time to make viewing more of a challenge. But that hasn't deterred the loyal fans.

During his rookie season, defensive tackle John Thornton fell behind on his soaps, so he began purchasing copies of *Soap Opera Digest* to catch up on the storylines. He got a better grip on his schedule as he adjusted to the NFL but was always selective. He watched *The Young and the Restless* and *The Bold and the Beautiful* religiously.

"I only watch the ones on CBS—you switch the channels and watch some of the soaps on the other stations and it's so obvious it's all fake," Thornton said. "Fake trees, fake background, and it's so easy to see. The scenery is so bad on the other stations that I never could get into the other ones."

Other players, of course, prefer to stick with sports on the tube during their break from the practice field. Others sleep.

Coaches would prefer them to watch film, but they understand.

> ## — TITAN TALK —
>
> "Heck, the way football is right now, it's good guys have a release, whether it's Jerry Springer or the soaps. You have to get your mind off football sometimes."
>
> —Jim Washburn,
> defensive line coach

SHARP DRESSER?

The Titans signed free agent Yancey Thigpen in 1998 to provide a big-play threat for years to come.

Injuries slowed Thigpen throughout his playing days with the team and limited his production. But he added something to the club: a sense of style.

In an informal poll conducted by *The Tennessean* in 1999, teammates voted Thigpen as the best dresser on the team. During that season he was even giving teammate Kevin Dyson tips on clothing—and Dyson actually listened.

But even Thigpen admits he might have gone overboard a bit when he wore a lime green jacket to and from the Oilers' game at Three Rivers Stadium in 1998. He roamed the field in the outfit before the game while chatting with old friends from the Steelers but changed out of it while he watched the game on the sideline because he was injured.

"I couldn't wear it on the sideline," Thigpen explained of his clothing change for the contest. "There might have been a glare, it might have messed with our players' vision."

BATTER UP

Training camp is a grind. More than three weeks of two-a-day practices in the grueling sun is enough to leave just about anyone's head spinning, especially rookies.

And every year it does, but for more than one reason.

Sure, the playbook is tough. But the dizzy bat race on the last day of training camp each year has left countless rookies falling all over the place.

Stooping over with their foreheads placed on the end of a baseball bat, the rookies get spun around and around and around by the veterans. Then the rookies are supposed to run to a football placed roughly 20 yards away, pick it up, and run back to the starting point, which is also the finish line. All the while, the veterans stand by and laugh as the disoriented rookies stumble around before regaining their sense of balance. Some remain disoriented longer than others.

It's great comedy after weeks of tension. And it can be pretty embarrassing, too.

"You can see that ball," punter Jason Bloom said. "But you just can't get to it. I just kept drifting further and further away."

— **TITAN TALK** —

"I felt like I had just drank a bottle of tequila."

—Zach Piller, guard

The dizzy bat race is a tradition that keeps the rookies grounded.
Donn Jones

Better Left Unsaid

Bruce Matthews moved from Houston to Nashville, but he certainly didn't forget "The Comeback Game." Neither did the five other members of the 1992 Oilers who became Titans in 1999.

Buffalo's 41-38 victory in the AFC Wild Card playoff game over the Oilers will always be a painful memory from the past. The Oilers led 35-3 in the second half of that game but blew it. It was the greatest comeback in NFL playoff history and arguably the lowest moment for the franchise.

So what's the best way to get off on the wrong foot with the old vets? Arrive on the team as a rookie and list the "Comeback Game" as your favorite NFL game of all-time.

That's exactly what three Titans' rookies—quarterback Kevin Daft, receiver Darran Hall, and safety Brad Ware—did when they filled out a questionnaire from the league at the NFL Symposium.

Word leaked out not long after they arrived in Nashville.

All three started scrambling when they were discovered, and they tried to save themselves with honesty. They simply explained they thought the game was exciting. Ware said he was actually a Bills fan back then and had a bet with his dad on the game. When the Bills were getting beat 35-3, Ware left the house because he couldn't stand the ribbing. When the Bills rallied, he ran back home, only to find the doors locked.

Daft ended up making the team's 53-man roster in 1999; Ware and Hall were released.

Worth the Grief

The picture of Kevin Dyson streaking down the sideline on the way to the end zone at the end of "Home Run Throwback" undoubtedly hangs on the walls of houses all across Tennessee.

Punter Craig Hentrich wouldn't mind seeing them put away, at least if it's the photo that ran on the front page of *The Tennessean* the next day.

Don't get Hentrich wrong—he loved the play. It helped the Titans beat the Bills and advanced them in the 1999 playoffs. But the goofy expression on his face set him up for tons of grief. In the photo, Hentrich was caught with his mouth wide open as Dyson ran by. The look on his face made him look as though he'd just been spooked.

"I've gotten more grief around here," he said. "Everyone has been making fun of the way I look. That was just sheer excitement. I lost all control."

PLANNING AHEAD?

When the Titans hired Ronnie Vinklarek as a defensive assistant prior to the 2000 season, he came with high marks from the team's defensive coordinator, Gregg Williams.

But with a smile, Williams also accused Vinklarek of brownnosing a little bit when it came to landing the job with the Titans.

Vinklarek's kids, after all, bear middle names that suggest he might have had his eye on the Titans and thought he needed something to tip the scales in his favor.

Vinklarek named his sons Trevor Reese Vinklarek and Trent Fisher Vinklarek. Sounds like someone was trying to win over the head coach and general manager.

"It kind of says you'll go to any lengths when you pick middle names of your sons, one for Jeff Fisher and one for Floyd Reese," Williams joked.

Vinklarek said he wanted the job, but no, didn't go to those extremes.

"Reese, that was my mother's maiden name," Vinklarek explained. "Fisher, that is my wife's mother's maiden name. But you know they aren't buying that here."

Don't Believe Everything You Read

Undrafted rookie safety Joe Walker didn't know whether to laugh or cry.

It didn't matter, because plenty of his family and friends were doing both for him when the Titans trimmed their roster to 53 players just before the start of the 2001 season.

Walker's head was spinning when his name was erroneously listed on NFL.com as one of the players the Titans had released. While he was getting ready to practice, friends were calling him from everywhere to express their condolences.

"I had a couple of guys call me and said they had seen it on the Internet," Walker said. "They were like, 'Sorry to hear about it.'

"I called them back and was like, 'Man, I've got some good news. ...'"

Still, Walker seemed on edge for a few days, almost like he wasn't sure what to believe.

He ended up remaining the entire season, playing in all 16 games, with three starts. But Walker was released by the Titans prior to the 2002 season, and that time it was no mistake.

Where's Your Car?

Titans safety Joe Walker loved his Mercedes. It was his pride and joy and his personal reward for making the team as a rookie in 2001.

The shiny new car was also a part of his nightmarish day that season.

Despite being surrounded by Pro Bowlers such as Blaine Bishop and Samari Rolle, Walker got a little too big for his britches as a rookie. Some of his teammates felt he was acting a little too flamboyant, and they knew just the way to get his attention: his car.

One day when Walker was in a meeting room, Rolle and safety Aric Morris got Walker's car keys out of his locker and moved his Mercedes out of the players' lot and out of sight into a parking lot across the street.

Strength and conditioning coach Steve Watterson then wrote a letter, complete with a Mercedes logo at the top, that stated that Walker's car had been repossessed because the dealership hadn't received payments. Listed on the letter was an address where Walker's car could be picked up.

A security officer, recruited to be a part of the scam, then delivered the bogus letter to Walker, who went into full panic mode as other players snickered behind his back.

Walker bolted to the parking lot and discovered his car was gone. As the hours passed, he began to get depressed.

At the end of the day, Walker pulled cornerback Andre Dyson aside and asked him for a ride. That's when Rolle decided the joke had gone on long enough, and he tossed Walker the keys.

Walker breathed a sigh of relief, and the other players never had any problems with him after that.

A Big Ogre

Josh Evans is a bear on the football field, but off it he's a very likeable guy.

Media members always found the Titans defensive tackle very approachable, and his fellow defensive linemen always had a lot of fun with him. Despite his trials and tribulations in dealing with the league's substance abuse policy (he was suspended twice during his playing days with the Titans), Evans always seemed to have a smile on his face.

Evans was even a good sport when teammate Keith Embray placed a Shrek doll in his locker during training camp in 2001. The next day, fellow defensive tackle Joe Salave'a's surprised Evans with a large cardboard stand-up poster of Shrek, the large green ogre that is the main character of the animated films.

Many of the Titans had convinced themselves Evans and Shrek looked a lot alike.

Evans laughed it all off. He usually fired back with practical jokes of his own.

"I guess because I carry myself with such prestige and highness these fellas feel like they have to make a joke about me. They can't find any flaws, so they have to say I look like [Shrek]," Evans said. "But you have to admit, he does have some cute eyes."

But when a reporter had the nerve to call the 275-pound Evans "Shrek" one day, the joke was over in a hurry. Evans wadded up the cardboard poster and shoved it into a nearby trashcan. The joke was over.

The 2001 season was the last one for Evans in a Tennessee uniform. Coincidentally, he ended up taking one more step in the Shrek direction, adopting green as his color when he joined the New York Jets.

> ### — TITAN TALK —
>
> "If you look at Josh and Shrek, they ain't too far apart."
>
> —Keith Embray,
> defensive end

EVERY DOG HAS HIS DAY

As a rookie, Titans receiver Justin McCareins didn't have the type of season he wanted, but at least he had someone with him to share the pain—his dog.

In his first NFL start against the Buccaneers, McCareins suffered a fractured left ankle. Three days later, he had surgery to have a pin inserted into the ankle.

Coincidentally, on the same day McCareins's dog, Spike, had ACL surgery on his knee.

Spike, a Rottweiler, was injured playing in the yard.

"When Justin's doctor found out about [Spike] he told him he should have brought the dog in and gotten a two-for-the-price-of-one," said Cliff Brady, McCareins's agent. "The vet said Justin should've come there for a two-for-one.

"The good news for the Titans is Justin is expected to be back before the dog."

Unfortunately for McCareins, the dog had better luck. When McCareins eventually returned, he re-fractured the ankle in practice and was lost for the season.

HAWAII BOUND!!!!????

There's the Pro Bowl, and then there's the Titans Scout Team Pro Bowl Player of the Year.

Both of them are quite an honor and result in a trip to Hawaii. Only one of them, however, is fake.

It's the second one, of course. That's one you certainly don't want to win.

But near the end of every season, at least one unsuspecting rookie gets picked. It could be a draft pick, a free agent, or even a practice squad player. If the guy has worked on the scout team in practice against the team's first unit, he's eligible.

He's eligible to become the butt of one of the biggest practical jokes of the season.

Not long after the Pro Bowl winners are announced around the league, the Titans quietly select the Scout Team Pro Bowl Player of the Year. They inform the player—who's always curious about this award he'd never previously heard of—that he gets to go to Hawaii to practice against the real Pro Bowl players the week of the game.

The "winners" are served up to members of the media who are also in on the joke. And usually the player is gushing. Defensive tackle Rien Long fell for it hook, line, and sinker in 2003, flashing a huge smile while answering each question. When he got back to his locker, defensive end Jevon Kearse congratulated him over and over again and began offering travel tips for his trip to the island. Long was all ears.

Cornerback Tony Beckham was a little more suspicious his rookie season, and he contends now he never believed the prank from the start.

In 2001, ecstatic receiver Chris Taylor immediately came into the locker room, picked up his cell phone, and called his agent, family, and friends. It was tough to watch.

The players aren't informed it's all a big hoax until a team meeting several days later when the entire team watches the bogus interview and roars.

Some of the victims get over it faster than others. It usually depends on how many folks they'd already invited to go to Hawaii with them.

TITANS FUNNIEST VIDEOS

When Kevin Carter drew the short straw one Halloween night, he had no idea it would be so costly.

Now he knows. Boy, does he know. Unfortunately, so do many of his teammates as well.

It sounded like a good idea at the time. Carter; his wife, Shima; and their little boy, Zion, all planned on going out in costumes. One would be a football player, one a referee, and the other a cheerleader.

They drew straws, and with the shortest one Carter—you guessed it—was the cheerleader.

And the six-foot-five, 290-pounder went all out. He put on a blond wig and eyeliner. He put on the tights, along with a stuffed bra, and a cheerleader's outfit, of course.

Then came the set up. The wife of teammate Zach Piller had heard of the Carter family outing. She called Shima, claiming she wanted a picture of young Zion for a scrapbook.

But when she slowly pulled up on the street with a camcorder, Carter knew he'd been had. There was nowhere to run.

"I was like, 'Oh crap,'" Carter said. "But I started hamming it up for the camera anyway."

Carter should have known it was a mistake. Days later, Titans coach Jeff Fisher had his hands on the tape. Carter's dirty little secret was exposed before the entire team the night before a game. The Pillers had done him in.

"There I was in a cheerleader's uniform," Carter said. "It was embarrassing, but it was all in fun, I guess."

PAY UP!

Titans coach Jeff Fisher shook his head and managed to break a smile.

Across the practice field, Titans center Gennaro DiNapoli was wet and shivering. Some of DiNapoli's teammates, meanwhile, were on their way to the nearest ATM machine—they needed money to pay off a bet.

Just a few days before Tennessee's *Monday Night Football* game in Pittsburgh in late October 2001, DiNapoli proved to everyone he might do just about anything on a dare, especially if money is on the line.

During a lull in practice on a blustery day, some of the Titan offensive linemen looked out over the manmade pond next to the team's practice facility and began proposing some crazy ideas. They ended up daring DiNapoli to swim across a roughly 40-yard stretch of water and then swim back.

No one thought DiNapoli would do it, of course. After all, the water was dirty and cold. And it was a crazy idea to begin with.

But DiNapoli was up for it. And when practice ended, he stripped down to shorts and a T-shirt and jumped in. As many of his teammates watched, DiNapoli swam from one shore to the other and back.

After DiNapoli dried off, he ended up collecting more than $1,500. Some of his teammates, however, didn't pay up as quickly as DiNapoli might have preferred.

"I was so pumped the water didn't seem all that cold," DiNapoli said. "Now I just need everyone to pay up. If they don't they might get clipped—I'm Italian, so I don't mess around."

A Nose for the Elbow?

The players were psyched and so were the coaches. The Steelers were in town for a big game, and during pregame warmups it seemed like players were going through drills at 100 miles an hour.

On one end of the field, Steve Watterson was doing his part to get the defensive linemen revved up.

Lined up as an offensive lineman, he worked with the players on a specific pass rush technique designed to get them to the quarterback. One by one the players passed through before defensive tackle Josh Evans stepped up.

He left his mark—literally.

While using the technique, Evans's elbow struck Watterson across the bridge of his nose.

"At first it stunned me, but it seemed like no big deal," Watterson recalled.

But it was. Witnesses said Watterson's nose was sideways on his face, broken and bleeding. Evans was nearly speechless when he turned around to take a look at the damage.

"The funny thing is, Steve just kept on going," said general manager Floyd Reese, who happened to be standing nearby. "You know how you think you'd grab your nose, go to your knees, all that stuff? Well, he never skipped a beat."

Watterson could've used stitches, but instead got his nose taped up with bandages and was ready for the game. In the days that followed he looked more like the team's mascot, T-Rac, with a pair of black eyes as souvenirs.

Location, Location, Location

A locker room is a home away from home for players in the National Football League.

During the season, the Titans spend countless hours at Baptist Sports Park. And while most of the days are spent on the practice field or in meeting rooms, they have to dress somewhere, and they need a place to keep their equipment and personal belongings. Exactly where is left up to the team's equipment manager, Paul "Hoss" Noska, who is a landlord of sorts. Seniority also has a lot to do with where a player's locker ends up in the locker room.

Some players like their locker spot, others aren't so sure.

Take, for instance, tackle Brad Hopkins. He inherited his locker when offensive lineman Bruce Matthews retired following the 2001 season. Many assumed it was an upgrade. Hopkins quickly found out otherwise. His locker, you see, is located next to a door that leads to a busy hallway.

"I am the first butt people see," Hopkins said. "If I am putting my socks on and haven't put my shorts on yet, 'Hello!' There is no advantage to being here."

Linebacker Peter Sirmon's locker is located next to the doors leading to the showers. Players regularly "borrow" his shampoo or snag his towel.

Most agree quarterback Steve McNair has the best locker. It's at the end of the locker room, and he has a spare locker next to his. Eddie George also has a prime spot, on an end with a little extra elbow room.

Guard Benji Olson wouldn't trade his spot for the world, though. He's next to the light switch and thermostat, and the same door that Hopkins likes to try and keep shut. It can have its advantages.

"I have more control [where I am]," Olson said. "Plus, I get to moon people a lot."

LAYING THE SMACK DOWN

In the NFL, defensive linemen are usually willing to do whatever it takes to get to the other team's quarterback.

If it's legal, they'll try it. Sometimes they push the limit.

But by now, Titans offensive linemen Fred Miller and Zach Piller probably feel like they're prepared to handle just about anything thrown their way—including folding chairs. Not to mention the wrath of their general manager, Floyd Reese.

Just two weeks before the start of training camp in 2002, Miller and Piller were among a handful of Titans on hand for the *Total NonStop Action* pay-per-view wrestling event in Nashville one July night. The players are both wrestling fanatics and buddies with National Wrestling Alliance wrestler Jeff Jarrett.

So the three came up with a plan beforehand that would allow Miller and Piller to have some fun and also be a part of the action. What transpired ended up being debated by everyone involved.

But hey, that's what wrestling is all about, isn't it?

"We didn't know exactly what we were going to do, but it was a setup," Miller said. "We said we were going to throw a couple of blows back and forth and try and make it look as real as possible."

So when Jarrett began taunting a group of Titans sitting at ringside, Piller and Miller did exactly what they thought they were supposed to do. They threw fake punches and pretended to get hit.

Things escalated when they jumped a barricade. That's when things got a bit more physical.

Even Jarrett admitted things "got out of hand" when the confrontation turned more physical.

Eventually other players and wrestlers jumped in and joined the action by throwing a few fake punches. There was more physical contact. Other wrestlers hit the players with folding chairs. Afterward, the players and wrestlers got together and laughed about it.

There was only one problem: Reese saw a replay of the action on the evening news, and he wasn't laughing.

"I am not real excited about seeing my guys jump over fences and get thrown into rings and get hit with chairs, I think that is probably fairly easy to understand," Reese said. "They will have plenty of time to wrestle when their football career is over. They have better things to do than just be wrestling with wrestlers. There is always a time and a place, and this is probably not the best time nor place."

The two players haven't wrestled since, at least not in public. And don't expect to see it happen any time soon.

"We are warned not to ride motorcycles or ski and stuff like that," Piller said. "I guess [Reese] will probably add wrestling to that list. I think that was my shot at greatness."

LEAVING IT ALL ON THE FIELD

Re-hydrate, replenish, and refuel. Those three words can be found across the bottom of bottles of Gatorade.

Only what happened during the end of one Titans practice probably isn't what the folks at Gatorade had in mind for their product.

Boredom got the best of a handful of Titans and a student manager in August 2002.

With their assignments completed and time running out on a night practice at the Coliseum, a group of offensive linemen challenged a student manager to drink what remained of a gallon of Gatorade concentrate. There was roughly half the bottle remaining, which when full and combined with water makes six gallons of Gatorade.

The deal was simple: If the manager could drink it and hold it down until practice ended, the linemen would pay him $500.

It sounded like such a good money-making opportunity that Titans defensive tackle Kris Kocurek, who was not practicing because of a shoulder injury, grabbed another bottle and said he wanted a piece of the action, too. He also would have to drink an entire bottle.

The manager and Kocurek downed the drink, but minutes later began turning a shade of lemon lime. At the same time, some players pretended to throw up, hoping to get a reaction from the drinking duo.

But no acting was needed. By the end of practice both had vomited—numerous times.

Their reward: an evil look from the head coach, who wasn't amused.

HE DESERVED A KICK IN THE PANTS

Titans offensive lineman Barry Hall dislocated the big toe on his right foot during a preseason game at Minnesota in 2002—that's undisputed.

Exactly how he did it, however, was up for debate, though it was pretty one-sided.

Sideline witnesses that night in the Metrodome said a frustrated Hall kicked a cart on the sideline after jumping over a table. He was attempting to make a tackle following an interception when he was shoved out of bounds.

When asked about it following the game, Hall gave this account:

"After I got pushed I saw the water table and it was either 'hit it or go over it,' so I jumped on the table and as soon as I landed, it was like fire," Hall said. "Then I bumped into the cart and I came back and my toe was broke."

By then, rumors were already spreading about Hall injuring the toe by kicking the cart, but Hall denied it.

Coach Jeff Fisher, however, was pretty straightforward when describing Hall's toe injury. He, too, had apparently heard that the cart was involved.

"Barry Hall has a dislocated large toe on his large foot as a result of a small brain, I guess," Fisher explained. "He said he did it before he kicked whatever he kicked—we'll talk to him, but it looks as though he injured his foot kicking something behind the bench."

Hall's practice time was limited in the following days because of the injury, and he ended up getting the boot himself. The team released him.

STRONG BONES

Clevan "Tank" Williams was smart enough to start at safety for the Titans in a complicated defensive scheme as a rookie in 2002.

It didn't take him long to prove he was tough enough as well. His back-jarring hit on Colts quarterback Peyton Manning was one of the most memorable hits of the 2002 season. It caused a fumble, which was picked up and returned for a touchdown by teammate Keith Bulluck in Tennessee's win in Indianapolis.

So Williams must have gotten his nickname "Tank" for his hard-nosed play on the football field, right? Well, not exactly.

"When I was a baby, I continuously drank bottle after bottle of milk," Williams explained. "So my mom said, 'Why don't you give him a tank of milk?'"

WHO ARE YOU CALLING PRETENDERS?

The Titans had heard enough.

They'd rolled off eight wins in nine games during the 2002 season, yet folks all over the country were questioning them, including ESPN analyst Sean Salisbury. He had the nerve to call them a playoff "pretender" on air.

Titans linebacker Keith Bulluck saw it. So did safety Lance Schulters.

After a win over the New England Patriots on *Monday Night Football*, they sounded off in the locker room.

"We've been called pretenders, fake, you know, all that stuff—mainly Sean Salisbury. I'll call him out. I'll put his a- - on blast," Bulluck said. "He's been talking s- - - about us all year."

*Keith Bulluck knows how to get back at TV sports
commentators and capture some of the limelight.*
Donn Jones

By the next morning, word had reached Salisbury, a former
NFL quarterback, that the Titans were upset with him. By midday,
Salisbury and Bulluck were both on air on the nationally syndicated
Dan Patrick Show on ESPN Radio.

Bulluck passed a cell phone around the locker room so Schulters and cornerback Samari Rolle could have their say on the matter, too.

"I had to release the hounds," Bulluck said.

Patrick tried to stir things up even more claiming Salisbury also called the Titans "soft." But Salisbury denied that claim. Ten minutes later, all parties were satisfied. And Salisbury jumped on the team's bandwagon.

"If I had known Keith and the guys were going to get this fired up," Salisbury said, "I would have said it early in the season. But I'm glad Keith and those guys are watching."

SOUP OF THE DAY

Titans strength and conditioning coach Steve Watterson is always looking for a chance to play a practical joke.

A year after Bengals running back Corey Dillon rushed for 246 yards against the defensive unit of then-Titans defensive coordinator Gregg Williams, Watterson planted a blown-up picture of Dillon's face on a tongue-depressor inside Williams's office aquarium. The words: "I ate your fish" were stretched out from Dillon's mouth.

When Williams went to feed his fish, he saw Dillon and he wasn't amused.

On another occasion, Watterson used a fake transaction notice to convince former Oilers defensive lineman Gary Walker that he'd been traded to the Washington Redskins.

Watterson's a mastermind of evil tricks.

But it was his spur-of-the-moment decision during a regular-season game against the Steelers in 2002 that ended up making him the butt of a joke around the complex and eventually got him in the .

headlines nationally before the two teams met again in the AFC divisional playoff game.

Steelers linebacker Joey Porter helped stir the pot. In the days leading up to the January 2003 playoff game, Porter accused Watterson of dumping a cup of hot liquid on him during a sideline scrum during the regular-season contest in Nashville. He singled out Watterson, sort of.

"I tackled Steve McNair before he went out of bounds, and as I tackled him and he was going out of bounds, that little bald-headed guy came over and threw some coffee on me and thought he was slick about it," Porter told reporters back in Pittsburgh. "He threw coffee on me and handed the cup to a player. I got it on tape. I seen it on tape."

When relayed Porter's claim, Watterson laughed it off. He even pretended to take offense to Porter calling him "bald headed and short" even though, to be perfectly honest, he's not tall and he doesn't have a lot of hair.

While Watterson denied he did anything wrong, TV replays were and still are suspicious, to say the least. In fact, Watterson's cup-pouring action was actually spotted by the team's video staff immediately after the regular-season game.

And some had a little fun at his expense, sending him a fake fine letter from the league with his name on it. Word is, Watterson even fell for it.

There was no Watterson-Porter incident in the playoff game, but Porter got his revenge in the long run when the two were reunited at the Pro Bowl in Hawaii following the season. That's when Porter dumped a five-gallon bucket of Gatorade on Watterson's head following the AFC's win over the NFC. Watterson was there with Tennessee's coaching staff.

"He goes, 'Now we're even,'" Watterson recalled. "We laughed about it, and I said, 'I don't know if we are really even. One little cup versus five gallons? Now I have to do some evaluation.'"

FORE!

Receiver Derrick Mason has gone through the middle of some pretty nasty defenses during his playing days.

He's been hit high and low, but usually he bounces right back up and keeps going.

Get him on a golf course, and things can get dangerous. Seriously.

Mason showed up at a May minicamp in 2003 with a splint on his right hand after fracturing a bone while hitting a golf ball. He was playing in a charity golf tournament. Mason said he hit behind the ball while teeing off with a driver.

Mason's teammates hardly cut him any slack, though he was spared some ribbing when another one of his teammates, defensive tackle Albert Haynesworth, showed up the same day limping. His excuse was he injured it by stepping wrong on a curb when getting out of his car.

SECOND TIME'S THE CHARM

The mood in the Titans' locker room was sour one June day in 2003. Some players were downright ticked off.

Minutes earlier, coach Jeff Fisher had informed the team that popular veteran linebacker Randall Godfrey had been released. This was after Godfrey had taken a significant pay cut in order to stay earlier in the off season.

Some players sounded off to the media while others discussed their frustration privately. No one liked the way it was handled by the club.

Cornerback Samari Rolle tried to lighten up the mood with a practical joke. He nearly ended up giving one of his teammates a heart attack.

While the player in line to claim Godfrey's old spot—Frank Chamberlin—conducted interviews, Rolle snuck up behind him and placed a long plastic snake on his shoulder. Chamberlin didn't flinch.

Rolle eventually got the reaction he was looking for, however, when he tossed the snake into the locker stall of young safety "Tank" Williams, who was busy putting back together an electric razor. Williams screamed and the razor fell to the floor as he bolted across the locker room. It turns out Williams had fallen for the same stunt earlier in the week.

BALL RETRIEVER

Punter Craig Hentrich adores his little girl, Abbey.

Pictures of Abbey hang in his locker at Baptist Sports Park, and her name is even tattooed on his leg.

Hentrich needed his daughter more than ever when he was a man without a contract for several months leading up to the 2003 season. As the Titans practiced, it was up to Hentrich to get ready on his own.

That's when Abbey went from being his daughter to his workout partner, even though she was just three years old at the time.

Father and daughter would head for an open patch of grass together. Daddy Hentrich would punt, and little Abbey would help him shag the footballs.

She seemed to work out just fine. In fact, her dad was excited about her potential.

"Next year, I am going to teach her how to snap," Hentrich said."

No word yet on how that's going.

*Craig Hentrich got a little help preparing for the
2003 season from his three-year-old daughter, Abbey.*
Donn Jones

FACE PLANT

As Indianapolis Colts cornerback Nick Harper slowly weaved his way back and forth across the RCA Dome turf before eventually crossing the goal line on his 75-yard interception return against the Titans in September 2003, no one was in much of a laughing mood.

The players saw Harper's return as a slap in the face or at the least an exclamation point to Indy's 33-7 win. They didn't like the fact he took his own sweet time to score, and they were embarrassed.

But a closer look at the play provided some comic relief after all, courtesy of Titans tackle Brad Hopkins.

As Hopkins ran after Harper, he accidentally stumbled on the turf and fell flat on his face. As it happened, some of his teammates noticed.

And Hopkins knew the heckling was coming. He had been guilty of what the offensive linemen call a *face plant*—when they fall and land face first.

In the film room a few days later, Hopkins was forced to watch his fall from grace over and over and over again. Whoever said, "What happens on the field, stays on the field," surely wasn't an offensive lineman.

A BIG HIT

Raised voices. Bruised egos. Stiff competition. High fives.

Yeah, it happens on the practice field every day. But on many days those same things can be found without even leaving the locker room, thanks to quarterback Steve McNair.

McNair surprised his teammates during the 2003 season with a Golden Tee golf video game, just like the one you might find at a game room or bar. He purchased it and had it placed in the players' lounge just off the locker room.

It was a huge hit, though many players steer clear when punter Craig Hentrich is involved in the game.

"Nobody can beat him," McNair said. "I'm not going to play him. He is not going to embarrass me."

OH DEER!

Fred Miller shot a deer and then became a movie star.

And by all accounts, the film got great reviews—from everyone but Miller, that is.

Here's the not-so-Hollywood script: Late in the 2003 season, the Titans offensive tackle used an off day to go deer hunting and ended up bagging a 12-point buck with a hunting bow and arrow.

He was pumped and proud. Until he found out he had drifted from land where he had permission to hunt onto private property next to Radnor Lake State Natural Area in Nashville.

Making matters even worse: Miller's hunting license had expired.

It turned out to be a little embarrassing for Miller, who received a warning citation and called the whole thing a "big mix-up."

But Miller received his stiffest punishment when he showed up at the facility. News of the incident spread after a story appeared in the local newspaper, and his teammates began giving him grief. It was just the start.

Not long after that Miller became the subject of a short movie put together by the team's video staff. He was featured on the front of a bogus brochure from *Home and Garden* in which his face was superimposed on a hunter. It was titled, "Home and Garden, Special Edition—Fred Miller's favorite yards to shoot deer in."

The biggest roar came during a team meeting when the entire team was shown a *60 Minutes*-like piece about "Violence in the Neighborhood." The star? You guessed it—Miller.

Former 49ers lineman and current CBS analyst Randy Cross, in town to work a Titans game, served as the show's host.

"The Titans are playing well enough that their playoff-bound team is making plans to practice on Christmas day. ..." Cross said in the clip. "This may be all well and good, but in Nashville, Rudolph is not safe. ..."

The video cut to teammates who pretended to be appalled at Miller's actions. While speaking, guard Benji Olson even pretended to get shot by a stray arrow, presumably from Miller's bow. Mixed in were scenes from movies such as *Bambi* and *The Deer Hunter*.

Miller still catches grief from time to time. It's probably safe to assume he won't get caught hunting without a license again. If he does, there's no telling what might be in the sequel.

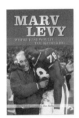

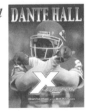